COOK.
NOURISH.
GLOW.

Originally published in the United Kingdom in 2015 by Michael
Joseph, an imprint of Penguin Books UK.

Appetite by Random House® and colophon are registered
trademarks of Penguin Random House LLC.

Library and Archives of Canada Cataloguing in Publication is
available upon request.

ISBN: 978-0-14753-019-6
eBook ISBN: 978-0-14753-020-2

Photography copyright © 2016 Susan Bell
Printed and bound in the USA

Published in Canada by Appetite by Random House®, a division of
Penguin Random House Canada Limited

www.penguinrandomhouse.ca

10 9 8 7 6 5 4 3 2 1

appetite
by RANDOM HOUSE | Penguin
Random
House

COOK.
NOURISH.
GLOW.

Amelia Freer

PHOTOGRAPHY BY SUSAN BELL

appetite
by RANDOM HOUSE

"I'M NOT ON A DIET,
I'M JUST EATING
HEALTHY, REAL FOOD."

Amelia Freer

For Mum
x

It's hard to believe that it's a year since *Eat. Nourish. Glow.* was published. I could never have imagined that so soon afterward I'd be creating my very own cookbook! I have been overwhelmed by the response to my first book and it has been a joy every day to know how many of you have embraced my principles of healthy eating. It has been so humbling for me to read your individual stories and to know that you have been making changes with such dramatic positive results for your health.

The many letters and emails I receive have had one very clear common thread: the need for more recipes. Rather than asking me about weight loss or superfoods, readers have written to me begging for more recipe ideas. And this makes me very happy indeed. Your kitchens have been detoxed, you have become graceful around food, you are moving your bodies in a way that you enjoy and you are glowing! How fantastic. It's a dream come true for me. And so it is with absolute delight that I am now delivering what you have asked for—a whole book filled with recipes that are dedicated to defending your health.

In this book I've remained true to everything that *Eat. Nourish. Glow.* offered, and I've built on those principles to provide practical, nourishing and delicious recipes. I hope you enjoy them and continue to bring healthy eating into your homes and lives and to celebrate good food while nurturing your health. I also hope there's something in this book for everyone, whatever cooking skills you have.

I love cooking and, ever since I began studying nutrition in 2004, I've been drawn to fresh ingredients and discovering and coming up with new recipes. I especially enjoy entertaining and serving beautiful food to friends and family. I'm not a trained chef, I'm a home cook and a genuine foodie. I can't stand bland, repetitive meals so my recipes have evolved out of necessity—I'm always looking for creative ways to provide my body with the goodness it needs to help me live the richest life possible. And by rich I mean healthy, happy and alert. As a nutritional therapist, my focus is on creating flavorful recipes that are packed with the most nourishing range of ingredients possible. Trust me, your body will thank you for eating these dishes.

I am evangelical about the difference eating well can make to your mind, body and health because my life changed when I changed my eating habits. I spent my twenties in a food rut. I was working long hours in an enjoyable but demanding job; I filled my days with endless cups of sugary tea, ate preservative-packed sandwiches for lunch and supermarket ready-made meals at night. I didn't think of myself as an unhealthy eater because I wasn't gorging on McDonald's every night, but those microwaveable lasagnas were just another form of fast food and the impact on my health and well-being was terrible. I felt exhausted all the time;

"THERE'S NO ONE GIANT STEP THAT DOES IT. IT'S A LOT OF LITTLE STEPS."

I suffered terrible IBS; dreadful acne and recurrent colds, infections and low mood. A visit to a nutritionist changed my life and I decided to study nutrition.

Over the years, as my relationship with food and its impact on my health has evolved, I've developed a fervent love of cooking. When I'm preparing food is truly when I'm at my happiest; I don't see it as a chore, rather as a therapeutic part of my day. Whether I'm throwing together a quick omelet for my breakfast or cooking a three-course supper for friends, I love every part of the process. I love playing with food, I love smelling it, chopping it up, throwing together different colors and finding new ways to serve up my favourite ingredients.

So when I began to consider writing a cookbook, I knew I wanted to write one that was true to my beliefs around food. Each and every person is different, but my experience working as a nutritional therapist has shown me that most people suffer inflammation as a result of eating too much grain, gluten, processed sugar and dairy, and so my recipes avoid these. I looked around at the cookbooks available and what I found was a very wide gap between gourmet food and convenience food. Several of my clients—and readers—think you have to choose one or the other. They wanted gourmet food when they had friends coming over for dinner or when they were eating out, and they reverted to quick and processed foods like cereal, toast, pasta, ready-made meals, packaged foods and stir-in sauces the rest of the time. So I started thinking about the middle ground. Meals you cook from scratch but that don't take hours or require fancy skills. Breakfasts you can throw together before work, dinners you want to eat when you walk in from a busy day. Basically real food for real life. And I call this process "food assembly."

I find that many of my clients, when I first start working with them, feel daunted by the prospect of having to spend hours in the kitchen and think they will need to cook complicated meals. That's why I prefer the term "food assembly." I don't aspire to create gourmet cooks and I, therefore, encourage my clients to take small steps, building on their skills. We live busy lives and I promise you I'm not going to ask you to spend hours slaving away in the kitchen. You can if you want to, of course, but this book has been designed to show that you can eat well in minutes if that's all you have. There are also recipes here to entertain family and friends, as well as giving you some therapeutic "me time" in the kitchen; these meals will take a bit longer to prepare but the results will be more than worth it. And I really do hope that any recipes I share with you in this book can be building blocks and inspiration for you. After all, we each have our own needs, likes and dislikes, and time restrictions.

I think we've been dumbed down by a convenience food industry desperate to keep us out of our kitchens and hooked on sugary, addictive, plastic-wrapped substitutes for real food that are almost totally devoid of nourishment. The key to taking back control over your health and well-being is to eat meals prepared from scratch, so you know exactly what has gone into them and you know that everything passing your lips will be working for you, not against you. We have been stripped of our confidence when it comes to food. We no longer trust our instincts; we are afraid of experimenting in case it goes wrong. I want to encourage people to just give it a try. Set aside some time to invest in cooking and caring for yourself. You deserve it. It is the best form of self-care I know. And you will be blown away by the difference it makes.

We are all in a relationship with food and it is our longest, most powerful and most intimate relationship. I know from experience how this relationship can shift to something quite toxic and damaging. Food can often be my clients' primary stressor in life. But I passionately believe that even the most toxic relationship with food can be turned around. There is always a reason behind a challenging relationship with food, and we need to better understand our emotional needs if we want to improve it once and for all. Starting from our mothers' breast milk, our first taste of food equates in our minds with love. We are programmed to seek pleasure and avoid pain, and food can be the swiftest, easiest form of love available to us.

I do not support an obsession with healthy eating at all—it's just about eating real food and understanding what that can do for our health. There are so many unhelpful nutritional beliefs out there that sometimes I think our quest for perfection can tend toward self-abuse. We lurch from fad to fad, never allowing ourselves to feel at home with our own eating. So as you embark on a journey to well-being with the recipes in *Cook. Nourish. Glow.* I recommend that you:

- **Pay attention to the quality of food, not the amount.** I am all for great taste and great nutrition sitting side by side at my table—kitchens are the hearts of our homes and that's where the healing happens.

- **Forgive yourself the odd mistake.** I unconditionally accept my clients no matter what their weight, their state of health or their issues with food—if a child falls, we give that child a hug, we don't tell him or her off. Self-acceptance is so important on this journey to becoming healthier—take it one step at a time.

- **Let the food teach you.** Your body will tell you which foods are right for you and which meals will have you bouncing out of bed in the morning—just listen.

- **Remember: human beings are meant to cook.** Industry processes. Step away from the ready-made meals and set time aside to invest in cooking yourself nourishing meals.

- **Think beyond your supermarket.** In order to be healthy, we do have to be a little bit savvy with how and where we shop sometimes. Farmers' markets sell ingredients, not meals, and you couldn't ask for a better source of ingredients for the recipes in this book. And yes, a lot of my recipes do involve a few more unusual ingredients. I know this can put people off; it's easy to think that if you can't buy it at your local shop, then it's impossible. That's not the case. I really recommend doing an online order of the healthier substitutes and stocking up on the right things in order to truly embrace the recipes in this book—don't feel that they are beyond you, because they aren't.

- **Get creative.** I want to encourage more diversity in your kitchens and better intuition when shopping—being more receptive to the smells, colors and feel of foods. After all, the act of eating is a fundamental part of life, yet we give such little attention to this most important stage: how we select our food. We so often get into bad habits picking the same things to put in our shopping cart week after week. So choose different colors, buy something you've never tried before, change where you shop, try out a new market or even take a new route home from work to pass by a different shop . . . Success in the kitchen really does start with shopping first.

- **Take it one step at a time and lean on your friends and family to help you change for good.** Healthy eating is so much more than just following a clean diet. It's how we shop, who we live with, who we share our food with and how we think about food. Being angry about it negates the goal! Ultimately it has to become a way of life, and so we do need support from those around us to make these changes.

Perhaps the most important reason why I decided to write this book is that I believe cooking is without doubt the most important thing we can do for our health. And however we do it, we must stop sleepwalking toward our utter dependency on processed and factory-made food. We must wake up and resist the food manufacturers' attempts to make us believe we don't have the time or skill to prepare food from scratch. We do! So I hope this book restores your kitchen confidence and helps you create enjoyable food for yourself and your loved ones. Because you deserve nothing less.

Enjoy!

Chapter 1

KITCHEN CONFIDENCE

Chapter 1 /
KITCHEN CONFIDENCE

Broccoli and cashew steam-fry

Cucumber noodles with tahini dressing

Spicy carrot salad

Roasted peppers with baked eggs

Spiced shrimp with spinach and coconut

Steam-fried cabbage with poached salmon

Steam-fried leeks with a steamed egg

Boy George's steamed asparagus
with pumpkin-seed salsa verde

Brussels sprouts, bacon, turnip and apple
with poached eggs

Stuffed beefsteak tomatoes

Poached chicken, crunchy vegetables
and herb dressing

Poached fish with spinach in
chili-tomato sauce

Poached Thai salmon with bok choy

If there's one message I want readers to take away from this book it's this: if you're looking to nourish your mind and body in the most efficient and nurturing way, then get into the kitchen with a few simple, delicious ingredients and COOK!

We currently know more about superfoods, calories, fat content and food groups than ever before. Yet obesity—and all the awful illnesses that go with it—is more prevalent than ever. So where are we going wrong? And what can we do about it? Well, as one of my favorite experts, the brilliant Dr. Mark Hyman, a physician and bestselling wellness author, said, "We have to cook our way out of this mess." And this starts with getting back in the kitchen and making all of our meals from scratch.

Cooking shows have, ironically, never been more popular. Yet so many of us are still relying on packaged cereal every morning (maybe with some token fruit thrown on top), buying pre-prepared soups and sandwiches every lunchtime and boiling pasta at night or pouring a ready-made sauce over meat and calling it cooking.

I'm not judging or belittling. I used to do all of these things myself. Every morning on my way into work I grabbed a croissant from a local café. At lunchtime I bought a ready-made sandwich, and every evening I slumped in front of the TV with a bowl of pasta or a stir-fry made with ready-made noodles and ready-made sauce. And I thought my diet was OK because I wasn't eating what I thought of as fast food, like pizza and burgers. In reality I was simply eating a slightly healthier kind of fast food. The ingredients were a little less bad for me than a take-out burger and the packaging was a little nicer. But my food was still fast and low on nutrients, and it certainly wasn't as alive as real, fresh food is.

So I don't judge anyone who eats this way because I've been there too. Back then I convinced myself I simply didn't have time to cook (a lot of my clients tell me this when they first come to see me). I had too much going on with work, my social life and my family. How on earth was I supposed to find time to cook? But this was just an excuse. I did have time—I just didn't have the basic skills needed or any "kitchen confidence," nor did I have the inclination—I'd fallen into the trap of believing that convenience food was a great invention made to make life better.

I put a lot of the blame for our current lack of "kitchen confidence" firmly at the door of the food manufacturers. For years they've tricked us into believing that cooking from scratch takes too long, or that it's too difficult. They fool us into thinking delicious food takes hours to prepare and that therefore it's far better to buy their over-processed, overly complex and artificially enhanced products instead.

So rather than whipping up a quick meal from scratch, we are enticed to buy a plastic tray with a beautiful picture on the front in the belief that it will be quicker, tastier and satisfying (once you know how easy and delicious some cooking can be, you'll never look at those ready-made meals again). And rather than whipping up a huge batch of fresh soup that will last for weeks in the freezer, we buy a plastic tub of overpriced soup that has been made months ago and preserved to the point where virtually all the vitamins and minerals have vanished.

We've been conned into thinking that cooking is hard and that all those brightly colored "packages and promises" lining the supermarket shelves are there to make our lives easier. But they're not. They're there to make the food manufacturers rich and they've been making us overweight and unhealthy and they've undermined our kitchen confidence.

So how do we start to cook our way out of this mess? Well, first of all, let's banish the word "cooking" and call it "food assembly." Because that's all it really is—you're just putting food together in a way that tastes great and nourishes your body. Second, just as I encourage clients to give up one thing at a time (whether that's sugar, soda or gluten), I advise a similar step-by-step approach to food assembly. Rather than vowing to now cook all your meals from scratch, start with one meal and build up from there. Very soon it will just become part of your day.

When I first became a nutritional therapist I knew all about food but little about food assembly. But then I started throwing a few ingredients together and found I could do it. I didn't follow long and fussy recipes. I simply took a few basic ingredients and experimented, tweaking my recipes as I became more confident or to suit my tastes. And I figured out early on that all you really need to make a great meal are three basic principles:

1. **Choose your protein and vegetables:** Your protein can be chicken, beef, pork, lamb, turkey, duck, egg, seafood, beans, nuts or seeds. Just keep it as organic, ethical and locally sourced as possible. For your vegetables, choose anything you love—again, as far as possible choose organic, local and seasonal produce.

2. **Find your flavor:** This is so important in food assembly. The food manufacturers know how palatable flavor is, so they pump their products full of artificial flavoring and/or sweeteners. But you can add lots of beautiful, natural, real flavor to your meals with anything: lemons; garlic; chili; fresh, dried or frozen herbs; fruits and vegetables; and oils, like coconut oil or olive oil. (Chapter 2 will help with this.)

3. **Assemble:** Last, put it all together. There are several cooking methods I encourage clients to use when assembling their food, as follows:

STEAM-FRYING

Originally a Chinese method of cooking, this combines both frying and steaming. A small amount of cooking is done first by frying (mainly the surface area of the food) and the majority of the cooking is then done with steam. You start by heating some oil (I use coconut oil) until hot and sauté the food for a few minutes until it starts to sizzle. Then add liquid (water, stock, wine, etc.) so that the food starts to stew or poach (instead of frying). Cover the pan so the steam is trapped and begins to cook the food. If the liquid evaporates before the food cooks, add a little more, put the lid back on and continue to cook. This way, food remains lovely and tender rather than overcooking.

POACHING

Poaching cooks food beautifully and leaves it very tender. Bring a covered pan of water to a boil and add your favorite flavors (like garlic or herbs). Then add your meat or fish or vegetables, put a lid on and remove from the heat to leave it to slowly cook through. Chicken takes around 25 minutes whereas fish takes less time (you'll know when something is cooked through as it will be piping hot throughout). As the food poaches, it holds on to the moisture and flavor from the water, leaving it wonderfully succulent. I often poach in big batches and then, when the meat or fish has cooled, shred it by hand and keep it in the fridge to add to salads later.

BAKING

This is dry-cooking in an oven and can be used for anything: fish, meat, vegetables and cakes. Certain foods (like fish) will cook quickly, whereas others (like stews) benefit from a long slow cook.

GRILLING

This method can really enhance the flavor of food and involves applying direct heat. Like baking, it can be used to cook meat, fish, vegetables, cheese or even eggs (you can finish off an open omelet or frittata by popping it under the broiler for a minute).

SAUTÉING

This involves heating oil (again, I love using coconut oil) in a pan; you then add vegetables and let them "sweat" (but don't blacken them).

Then eat! Ideally do this with family and friends, rather than in front of the laptop or TV. Whether you live alone or share your home, the basic act of sitting down to focus on the food you eat is a crucial part of digestion. Concentrate on your food, chew it thoroughly, breathe properly and stop when you're full. Eat mindfully.

I don't believe that any of the meals in this chapter, or in fact this book, need to be eaten at a specific mealtime, i.e. breakfast, lunch or dinner. I think you can eat any dish at any meal. I don't want to dictate that breakfast needs to be eggs or cereal or that supper needs to be fish and vegetables—I think that we have become too fixated on certain meals. If you want to eat broccoli for breakfast or fish soup, then by all means go ahead—let's break the boundaries of how we use and think about food. It is only our minds that tell us it's not normal to eat chicken in the morning.

The one thing finally holding you back from getting into the kitchen might be a lack of enjoyment when it comes to cooking—or food assembly! When I first speak to new clients about the importance of making meals from scratch, many admit that they simply don't enjoy cooking. But I find this is a mindset you can overcome, rather like when people say they "just don't like exercise." Often it's the thought of exercise they don't like, or a bad memory of never being picked for a team at school still lingers. Yet when they actually do it, they love it—especially the boost of feel-good endorphins and personal satisfaction they get after a run or exercise class. And it's often the same with food assembly.

Before I became a nutritional therapist I saw cooking as something to rush through before I could go and watch TV, but now I see it as my precious "me time," essential for winding down after a busy day. As my confidence in the kitchen has grown—and as I've seen the direct link between the foods I eat and how great my body feels—I've started to really enjoy being in the kitchen. I'll put music on, pick my protein, my vegetables and my flavors, and then I'll start tearing and chopping and blending. I love the smells and the sounds and watching a meal come together. And it really doesn't matter what it looks like or how it turns out. You can't really go wrong with simple ingredients, so go with the flow and see what you create.

Sometimes I'm in the kitchen for five or ten minutes; at other times an hour or more. I have days when I need to pull a meal together in ten minutes and others when I can spend half an hour or more puttering around. Similarly, some evenings I want something quick and deliciously simple, and other days I take my time. The point being that food assembly can take as long or as little time as you want it to. Just as you don't need to go to the gym for an hour every night to be healthy, you don't have to make a laborious meal every night either. In the same way as you might go for a run one day and then do a few minutes of stretching before bed the next, you can cook something a little more complicated one day and something incredibly simple the next. Whatever your skills in the kitchen or your time commitments, you can always find the time to make your meals from scratch.

I know this for a fact because readers of my first book have written to me in the thousands excitedly telling me how doing so has completely transformed their health. And the most startling thing they've found is how easy it is when they let go of the idea that they need the food manufacturers to do their cooking for them.

They've also told me how their families are now involved in the process too. Rather than sending their children off to play or watch TV while dinner is being made, mums have written to tell me how they now get their little ones involved. Others have written to say they've started cooking in the evening with their partner, each choosing their favorite recipes and taking turns cooking, rather than one popping something in the microwave. Cooking has the beautiful ability not only to transform a family's health but also to pull a family together in a wonderful way.

So ignore the phony rules and the plethora of packages and promises, get out of those central aisles in the supermarkets and head into your kitchen to make your meals from scratch. I promise you, it will be the single best thing you ever do for your health.

"DON'T BUY
MEALS, BUY
INGREDIENTS."

BROCCOLI AND CASHEW STEAM-FRY

This is a recipe for when you don't have any meat or fish in your fridge but you want to rustle up a filling meal, using nuts as a source of protein. A steam-fry is a healthy alternative to a stir-fry.

Cashews are a source of omega-3 fatty acids and, with a nice creamy flavor, they lend themselves well to this sort of dish. Broccoli has been found to be one of the most potently powerful foods for influencing our health positively, so I say wherever you can get it into your diet, do—daily, if possible.

So this is an anything-goes recipe, using whatever you might have in your fridge. Simply chuck in some nuts for flavor and you have a meal. If you can't afford, or choose not to eat, meat or fish, this is a quick tasty meal packed full of protein and veg. Other flavor combinations that work well are almonds and cabbage, green beans and pine nuts or kale and walnuts.

INGREDIENTS

coconut oil
1 head of broccoli, broken
  into florets (approx. ½ pound florets)
2 handfuls (approx. ½ cup) of cashew nuts,
  soaked in water for 1 hour
a ¾-inch piece of fresh ginger, peeled
  and finely sliced
a good splash of coconut aminos
  or tamari
sea salt or pink Himalayan salt
optional: chili flakes

Put 1 teaspoon of coconut oil into a frying pan on a medium heat. Add the broccoli florets and 2 tablespoons of water.

Drain the cashews and give them a quick rinse under fresh cold water, then add them to the pan with the ginger and the coconut aminos or tamari.

Mix well and steam-fry for 3 to 4 minutes (you want the broccoli to be crunchy, not soft), tossing the pan frequently. Serve with a little salt and chili flakes, if desired, and eat immediately.

SERVES 4 AS A SIDE DISH

CUCUMBER NOODLES WITH TAHINI DRESSING

This is such a delicious hit of flavor. It's a simple salad or a side dish, especially good with a barbecue, yet because it contains vegetables, fats and protein, it's also a complete meal by itself. It's so refreshing and light: perfect for the summer. I love the texture of the cucumber in noodles. It's a much more interesting way to serve it.

INGREDIENTS

1 small or ½ a large cucumber, washed
juice and zest of 1 orange
4 teaspoons tahini
optional: 1 teaspoon honey
a small handful of fresh mint, chopped
12 chive stalks, finely chopped
2 sprigs of fresh flat-leaf parsley, chopped
a pinch of sea salt
a large pinch of toasted sesame seeds

Use a spiralizer or peeler to make noodles out of the cucumber.

Mix the orange juice and tahini together. Add the honey (if using). Pour this dressing over the cucumber ribbons. Scatter the mint, chives and parsley over the top and stir well. Sprinkle with the sea salt, toasted sesame seeds and orange zest.

SPICY CARROT SALAD

This is a simple and quick salad to make, another recipe that came to be on a hungry night with an empty fridge. Sometimes the most delicious meals can be created at these times, using the simplest of ingredients. I'd happily eat this on its own, but it's also a lovely salad to serve with fish or as part of a salad buffet. It is so *delicious*!

INGREDIENTS

2 medium carrots, peeled
2 teaspoons fish sauce
juice of 1 lime
optional: a drizzle of toasted sesame oil
6–8 drops of Tabasco sauce, or to taste
1 small teaspoon raw honey
1 teaspoon melted coconut oil
optional: 2 tablespoons pumpkin seeds,
    olive oil, sea salt

Grate the carrots into a bowl. Add the fish sauce, lime juice, sesame oil (if using) and Tabasco. Massage in the honey and warm coconut oil with your hands.

If serving with pumpkin seeds, heat a pan and add the seeds to it when hot. Shake the pan until they pop, then add a drop of olive oil and some salt. Shake the pan again, then scatter the pumpkin seeds over the salad and mix well.

Voilà!

ROASTED PEPPERS WITH BAKED EGGS

For years one of my favorite quick meals was roasted peppers stuffed with feta cheese and harissa; this is now one of my boyfriend's favorite dishes and he makes it all the time. However, as I rarely eat feta, I wanted to come up with something else to stuff inside these delicious peppers. I tried an egg and—lo and behold!—it worked. It's great to eat at any time of the day. You can cook up a few in batches and keep them in the fridge to eat cold. It's a no-fail, great make-ahead recipe. Get creative and see what else you can stuff inside that pepper!

INGREDIENTS

1 large fresh pepper, washed, halved and seeds removed
olive oil
8 sun-dried tomatoes, finely chopped
2 teaspoons harissa paste
a handful (approx. 1 oz.) of fresh baby spinach, roughly chopped
sea salt and freshly ground black pepper
2 eggs, preferably free-range or organic
a small handful of fresh basil leaves, finely shredded

Preheat the oven to 350°F.

Put the pepper halves on a baking sheet, drizzle with a little olive oil and roast for 10 minutes.

Meanwhile, mix the sun-dried tomatoes and harissa paste together in a medium-sized bowl. Add the spinach and combine. Season with salt and pepper.

Remove the peppers from the oven. Spoon the tomato and spinach mixture into the peppers. Use the spoon to make a well in the center, then break a whole egg slowly over the top of each half (take care not to let the egg spill over). Return to the oven and bake for 16 to 18 minutes, until the egg yolk is cooked as you like it. I like mine just a little bit runny.

Sprinkle with a little shredded basil before serving.

SPICED SHRIMP WITH SPINACH AND COCONUT

I love shrimp because they're so versatile and quick to cook. This is a really simple meal that you can rustle up in minutes. But, as is always key with any quick meal, don't skimp on the flavor. Here I've given you a lovely mix of spices that will satisfy your taste buds.

INGREDIENTS

For the spice mixture:
2 teaspoons coriander seeds
2 teaspoons cumin seeds
1 teaspoon caraway seeds
¼ teaspoon spicy red pepper
  flakes or crushed chili flakes
sea salt

10 ounces raw jumbo shrimp, peeled
coconut oil
¼ pound baby spinach
a small handful of fresh cilantro,
  roughly chopped
½ cup coconut yogurt
zest and juice of 1 small lemon
freshly ground black pepper

To make the spice mixture, put the coriander seeds, cumin seeds, caraway seeds, pepper (or chili) flakes and a generous pinch of sea salt into a mortar and pestle and pound together until you have a fine powder. Alternatively, if you have a hand-held blender with a jar attachment you can use this. Add to the shrimp in a large bowl and toss together to evenly coat them in the spices.

Heat a medium non-stick frying pan over high heat and add 2 tablespoons of coconut oil. Add the shrimp and cook for 3 to 4 minutes, turning frequently until they turn pink and are cooked through. Remove the shrimp from the pan and set aside.

Return the pan to medium heat, add another tablespoon of coconut oil and wilt the spinach for 1 to 2 minutes. Stir in the chopped cilantro. Lower the heat and return the shrimp to the pan. Stir in the coconut yogurt, lemon zest and juice and season to taste with salt and pepper.

Cook for 1 to 2 minutes until the sauce is creamy and slightly thickened, then remove from the heat and serve immediately.

STEAM-FRIED CABBAGE WITH POACHED SALMON

This is my go-to evening meal when I'm tired and not much in the mood for cooking. But do not take that to mean it's a lesser recipe, because it's a success every single time I make it and utterly delicious. It doesn't matter if you don't have cabbage—just use any leafy greens. Put it all into the pan, add the salmon, pop the lid on and go and put your slippers on. This also works brilliantly for breakfast or lunch.

INGREDIENTS

coconut oil
½ pound white or red cabbage, shredded
2 wild salmon fillets, skin removed
zest and juice of ½ a lemon
1 jalapeño pepper, finely chopped
  and seeds removed
1 tablespoon capers, drained and rinsed
a small bunch of fresh parsley, leaves
  picked and roughly chopped
sea salt and freshly ground black pepper

Heat a frying pan and put in 2 teaspoons of coconut oil and 2 tablespoons of water. Add the shredded cabbage, mix well and put the lid on for 3 minutes.

Place the salmon fillets on top of the cabbage, adding 2 tablespoons more water if necessary. Put the lid on again for 5 to 6 minutes, and check occasionally to make sure the cabbage isn't sticking to the bottom of the pan. If it is, add a splash more water.

Once the salmon is cooked, add the lemon zest and juice, jalapeño, capers and parsley to the pan.

Season with sea salt and black pepper and serve the salmon on top of the cabbage.

STEAM-FRIED LEEKS WITH A STEAMED EGG

This is another favorite of mine that can be eaten at any time of the day! I love this dish, as it's not prescriptive and can be made with any greens in place of the leeks, but there is something lovely about the sweetness of the leeks paired with the egg. The tarragon and Tabasco just finish it off and bring it all to life with a bit of magic. If you can't get hold of any tarragon, fresh chives work well too.

I love the concept of a one-pan dish where you start off with all the flavors and pop an egg on top to steam. To me, this is one of the most comforting meals I could ever eat.

INGREDIENTS

olive oil
2 small leeks, washed and trimmed, sliced down the middle, then sliced into half circles, around ¼ inch thick
1 egg, preferably free-range or organic
sea salt and freshly ground black pepper
8 fresh tarragon leaves
Tabasco sauce

Place a small lidded frying pan on low heat then put in 1 teaspoon of olive oil and 2 tablespoons of water. Add the leeks and mix well, letting them sweat for 2 to 3 minutes—keep an eye on them and make sure they do not burn. Turn down the heat if they start to fry, otherwise they will taste bitter.

Once they have softened, use a spoon to make a small well in the leeks in the center of the pan and crack an egg into it, taking care not to break the yolk. Put the lid back on and let the egg cook for approximately 6 to 8 minutes, until the yolk has reached the desired texture.

Before serving, season with salt and pepper, sprinkle with fresh tarragon leaves and finish off with a splash of Tabasco.

BOY GEORGE'S STEAMED ASPARAGUS WITH PUMPKIN-SEED SALSA VERDE

This is a salsa verde that Boy George often makes, and since he shared his recipe with me, I now make it all the time too. As is his generous nature, he has shared it with us all. We had a lovely time making it (and eating it) together.

INGREDIENTS

1 bulb of fennel, roughly chopped
3 tablespoons capers, or olives
 if you prefer
2 handfuls of pumpkin seeds
1 handful of fresh mint leaves
1 teaspoon nutritional yeast flakes
3 tablespoons extra virgin olive oil
1 large bunch of asparagus, trimmed
sea salt and freshly ground black pepper

First make the salsa verde. Put the fennel, capers (or olives), pumpkin seeds, mint and yeast flakes into a small food processor and pulse until smooth. Add the olive oil and pulse again until well incorporated—you might need to add extra oil to bring the salsa verde together.

Steam the asparagus for 3 minutes, then serve with the salsa verde drizzled over, or as a dip on the side. Season to taste.

BRUSSELS SPROUTS, BACON, TURNIP AND APPLE WITH POACHED EGGS

Brussels sprouts are abundant in valuable nutrients, such as vitamins C and K, folate and manganese. They work brilliantly alongside the other crunchy components of this dish, all bound together by the rich poached egg. Perfect for a chilly autumnal day.

INGREDIENTS

8 slices smoked Canadian bacon
½ pound Brussels sprouts
coconut oil
1 Granny Smith apple, peeled, cored
  and cut into 8 small wedges
2 small turnips, cut into ½-inch cubes
a pinch of sea salt
¼ cup apple cider vinegar
2 large eggs, preferably free-range
  or organic

Put the bacon into a large cold non-stick frying pan. Turn the heat to low and cook for 5 to 10 minutes, turning occasionally until crispy.

Blanch the Brussels sprouts in a large saucepan of boiling water for 2 to 3 minutes before lifting them out of the pan and into a bowl of iced water. (Keep the pan of water ready for blanching the turnip cubes and poaching your eggs.) Once the sprouts are cold, drain and set aside.

Use the bacon pan to cook the Brussels sprouts, wiping the bacon fat out first and adding 1 tablespoon of coconut oil. Stir the sprouts for 5 minutes and set aside. Add another tablespoon of coconut oil to the pan and do the same with the sliced and peeled apple, until golden and softened but still holding its shape. Set aside.

Blanch the turnip cubes in boiling water for 5 minutes until tender, then add to the large frying pan with a pinch of salt. While the turnips are crisping, poach your eggs in the pan of simmering water with the apple cider vinegar. Add the Brussels sprouts and apples back to the pan with the turnip and cook for another minute or two to warm through. Serve with the crisp bacon and a poached egg.

STUFFED BEEFSTEAK TOMATOES

This might look like a dish which requires lots of effort but trust me, it's a really simple way to enjoy these ingredients.

INGREDIENTS

4 beefsteak tomatoes (approx. ½ pound each)
olive oil
2 large shallots, finely chopped (approx. ½ cup)
1 star anise, broken into pieces
a pinch of sea salt
1 small bunch of chives, finely chopped
½ pound lean ground beef
¼ cup leftover cooked quinoa
roasted yellow peppers, blanched green beans or blanched spring onions
freshly ground black pepper
extra virgin olive oil

Preheat the oven to 350°F.

Slice off the tops of the tomatoes and discard them. Scrape the insides out with a spoon (keep this—it's very flavorful and useful for adding to tomato-based sauces or salsa). Put the tomatoes on a non-stick baking sheet.

Heat 1 tablespoon of oil in a medium frying pan over a low heat and fry the shallots very gently with the star anise pieces for 10 minutes, adding a pinch of salt. If the shallots begin to burn, add a small splash of water. Remove the star anise and put the shallots into a large bowl with the chives.

Using the same pan, fry the beef for 5 minutes until brown, breaking it up with a wooden spoon. When the meat is cooked, add it to the shallots and chives. Let the mixture cool a little, then add the quinoa, mixing it all together thoroughly.

Fill the tomatoes with the beef mixture and tap with a spoon to press it down. Drizzle a little olive oil on top and cook for 25 minutes in the oven.

Serve with roasted yellow peppers, blanched green beans or blanched spring onions. Grind some black pepper over and drizzle with extra virgin olive oil.

> "I WAS 32 WHEN
> I STARTED COOKING.
> UP UNTIL THEN
> I JUST ATE."
>
> JULIA CHILD, CHEF

POACHED CHICKEN, CRUNCHY VEGETABLES AND HERB DRESSING

I used to be put off poaching chicken as I feared it was more complicated than my simple fried version. But it's actually so much easier, because while the chicken poaches you can prepare the rest of the food. These days I often poach 3 or 4 chicken breasts at a time, then keep them in the fridge so I can toss them into salads over the following days. Poaching really helps to keep the moisture in the meat, so the end result is much more enjoyable than dried, overcooked chicken.

INGREDIENTS

For the dressing:
10 almonds (1 tablespoon), soaked
2 sprigs each of cilantro, basil, parsley and tarragon, leaves picked and stalks set aside
1 small clove of garlic, peeled
sea salt
½ cup olive oil

2 x 5-ounce chicken breasts
1 clove of garlic, crushed with skin on
1 teaspoon sea salt
a handful (approx. ¼ pound) of green beans
1 bulb of fennel
1 carrot
1 small zucchini
6 ripe cherry tomatoes, halved
freshly ground black pepper
lemon wedges, to serve

For the dressing, drain and rinse the almonds in fresh cold water, then pound them with the herbs, the garlic clove and a little salt. Slowly pour the olive oil into the mixture, stirring to combine.

Put the chicken breasts into a pan of cold water with the reserved herb stalks (from the dressing), the garlic and the salt. Bring the water to a simmer, turn off the heat and immediately cover the pan. Allow the chicken to sit in the hot poaching liquor for 20 minutes, until cooked through.

Bring a medium saucepan of salted water to the boil and blanch the green beans for 1½ to 2 minutes, then cool under cold running water. Transfer to a large mixing bowl.

Preheat the broiler. Shave the fennel bulb with a mandolin or peeler into thin slices and do the same with the carrot and zucchini. Add to the beans. Put the tomatoes on a non-stick baking sheet and under a preheated broiler for 2 to 3 minutes until softened. Add to the bowl.

Remove the chicken breasts from the poaching liquor. Thinly slice them and add to the bowl of vegetables. Toss together and season to taste with salt and pepper. Arrange the chicken and vegetables between plates and serve with the herby dressing and lemon wedges.

POACHED FISH WITH SPINACH IN CHILI-TOMATO SAUCE

I like this one because it's a one-pan dish—you will need a pan with a lid. You can use a can of tomatoes instead of making the purée if you wish, but puréeing the tomatoes produces a better result.

You don't need to be precise with the quantities for this dish at all—a handful of cherry tomatoes, add some onion, etc. The important thing is to have the lid to keep in steam and heat so you get a very nice lightly cooked fish. You don't want to overcook it. I've used hake but you can use any white fish like cod, sea bass, halibut or even salmon. It's simple but tasty, and the kind of thing you could easily rustle up for yourself or friends. You can use any green veg but it works well with fennel—sautéed in a pan or slow-baked, or added to the pan and cooked with the fish and tomatoes. This is a great one for a novice cook.

INGREDIENTS

olive oil
1 red onion, peeled and finely sliced
1 bulb of fennel, finely sliced
1 fresh red chili, finely sliced
  (deseeded for less heat, if you like)
2 cups tomato purée from fresh or canned
  tomatoes
2 handfuls (approx. 6 ounces) of cherry
  tomatoes, cut in half
sea salt and freshly ground black pepper
4 x 5-ounce white fish fillets, such as cod,
  hake or sea bass, skinned and pin-boned
½ cup black or green olives, pitted
a handful of baby spinach

For the topping:
2 tablespoons finely chopped flat-leaf
  parsley
1 small clove of garlic, peeled and finely
  chopped or grated
zest of 1 lemon, plus a squeeze of juice

Put 1 tablespoon of olive oil into a pan on a medium heat and sauté the onion, fennel and chili for 2 to 3 minutes, to soften. Add the tomato purée and cherry tomatoes. Simmer for a further 4 to 5 minutes. Season to taste with a little salt and pepper.

Arrange the fish fillets in the pan, on top of the tomato sauce. Cover with a lid and simmer for 8 to 10 minutes, or until the fish is cooked and starting to flake. Just before serving, carefully stir in the olives and baby spinach and heat for a further minute.

Meanwhile combine the parsley, garlic, lemon zest and juice in a bowl.

To serve, arrange the fish fillets on plates and spoon over the tomato sauce. Sprinkle with the herby topping, and add a squeeze of lemon juice to finish.

Enjoy this with some additional steamed greens.

POACHED THAI SALMON WITH BOK CHOY

This is a failsafe meal for any time of day. Make up lots in advance and eat it whenever you need something tasty, delicious and filling.

INGREDIENTS

coconut oil
2 shallots, finely chopped
2 cloves of garlic, finely chopped
  or grated
a thumb-sized piece of fresh ginger,
  peeled and finely chopped or grated
1 red chili, deseeded and chopped
1 lime leaf, finely shredded
1 stalk of lemongrass, finely chopped
2 cups fish or vegetable stock
2 salmon fillets, skinned
2 bok choy, leaves separated
1 small handful of fresh cilantro leaves,
  to serve

Heat 1 tablespoon of coconut oil in a medium saucepan and fry the shallots, garlic, ginger and chili for a few minutes to soften. Add the lime leaf and lemongrass to the pan and cook for another minute.

Pour in the stock, bring to a boil, then reduce the heat. Simmer gently for 10 to 12 minutes to infuse the flavors. Add the salmon fillets and allow to poach for 7 to 8 minutes over gentle heat. Add the bok choy leaves for the last minute of cooking.

Arrange the salmon fillets and bok choy in serving bowls and ladle the fragrant broth over—remove the lime leaf and lemongrass before serving. Garnish with the cilantro.

Chapter 2
IT'S ALL ABOUT TASTE

Chapter 2 /
IT'S ALL ABOUT TASTE

———————————————

STOCK
Chicken / Beef /
Vegetable / Fish

SAUCE
Creamy, crunchy white sauce
/ Coconut-oil "hollandaise" /
Walnut miso sauce /Stir-fry
sauce / Tangy herb sauce

SALSA
Salsa verde / Avocado
papaya salsa

GUACAMOLE

HOMEMADE
COCONUT BUTTER

HUMMUS
Puy lentil hummus /
Green hummus

GREEN HARISSA

TAPENADE

KALE AND ALMOND PESTO

DRESSING
Mustard dressing /
Lemon and garlic dressing

FROZEN HERB AND
SPICE MIXES

FROZEN HERBS IN OIL

FLAVORED OIL

FERMENTED FOOD
Kimchi

One of the most common complaints I hear from new clients is that they find healthy food bland and boring. There's this idea that packaged, processed convenience food tastes great and healthy food doesn't. And it's mainly for this reason that so many people find it hard to make the switch to better eating.

Clients often tell me that in the past when they tried to overhaul their diet they mistakenly believed they had to forgo all flavor in order to be healthy. So they switched from a diet full of fake, artificial flavor to a very plain and simple one. For example, they'd swap sugary cereal or granola with berry compote for plain oatmeal made with skim milk. Or a chicken and noodle stir-fry made with sauce from a jar for a simple chicken salad without any fat or flavor. Is it any wonder they tired of this way of eating and rushed straight back into the arms of the food manufacturers?

I'm here to spread the word that eating well means eating some of the most exciting, delicious food out there and it doesn't need to be complex. When you've weaned yourself off unnatural flavorings, your taste buds will be delighted and re-educated by the range and depth of tastes on offer from real food in its most natural form.

The key to eating healthily and at the same time enjoying scrumptious food is to add your own flavor. And once you know how to create clean, natural and nourishing flavor you'll never want to return to the fake kind because it will suddenly taste synthetic, sugary and salty in a way that your own nourishing homemade flavor doesn't. So with that in mind, here are my favorite kinds of flavor, which I always have in my kitchen . . .

STOCK

Also more trendily known now as bone broth, but whatever you call it, all kitchens need a big batch of stock in the freezer. I store mine as ice cubes, in plastic freezer bags and old soup containers so that I always have a handy source of flavor to add to stews, soups, casseroles, sauces and stir-fries. I love poaching meats and fish in homemade stock to subtly add lovely flavor during the poaching process. Stock is incredibly simple to make and, while it can seem like a lengthy undertaking the first time you make it, a lot of that time is spent simply leaving it alone to do its thing, so it requires very little effort on your part. Stock is a rich source of collagen, which is tremendously healing for an inflamed digestive system, joints and skin, and is packed with vitamins and minerals. It is, quite simply, one of the most healing foods I know of.

BASIC STOCK RECIPE

Here is a basic recipe for making stock, be it chicken, beef, vegetable or fish. The method is the same for all of them: put the ingredients into a pan, cover with water, simmer and drain. There are a couple of things that change between them—a few key ingredients and the cooking time—so make sure to check this before starting your stock of choice.

You'll find that the simmering times are quite vague (e.g., 4–12 hours, 1–2 hours). This is because I've included the minimum amount of time that the stock should cook, in case you're pressed for time, but a good rule of thumb is that the longer it simmers, the better—especially with the chicken and beef stocks.

A slow cooker is particularly useful for making stock as you can cook it overnight, or just leave it to do its thing without worrying about the stove.

METHOD

First, prepare the vegetables (see "Base Ingredients," opposite). Leave everything unpeeled—including the onions and garlic—as the skins increase the flavor, and scrub the carrots, celery and leek clean under cold water. Roughly chop the vegetables, then place in a large, heavy, lidded pan—or slow cooker—depending on your chosen cooking method.

Pour in the water so that the ingredients are just covered—you might need to add a little more. If you're using a slow cooker, simply switch on and leave. Otherwise, bring to a boil, skimming off any scum that rises to the surface, then cover and simmer gently for the specified amount of time (see opposite).

Drain and remove the ingredients from the pan or slow cooker using a slotted spoon, then carefully pour the stock through a fine sieve into a container. At this point, taste and add more salt if needed. Use immediately, store in the fridge for up to 3 days or freeze until needed.

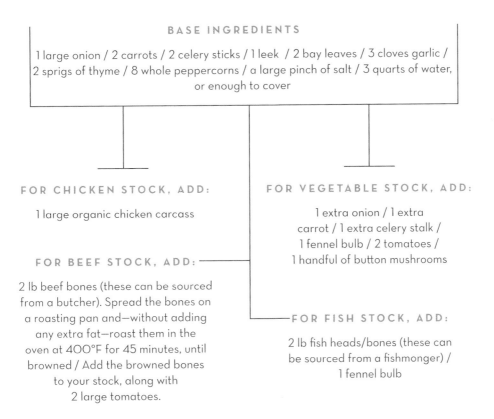

BASE INGREDIENTS

1 large onion / 2 carrots / 2 celery sticks / 1 leek / 2 bay leaves / 3 cloves garlic /
2 sprigs of thyme / 8 whole peppercorns / a large pinch of salt / 3 quarts of water,
or enough to cover

FOR CHICKEN STOCK, ADD:

1 large organic chicken carcass

FOR BEEF STOCK, ADD:

2 lb beef bones (these can be sourced
from a butcher). Spread the bones on
a roasting pan and—without adding
any extra fat—roast them in the
oven at 400°F for 45 minutes, until
browned / Add the browned bones
to your stock, along with
2 large tomatoes.

FOR VEGETABLE STOCK, ADD:

1 extra onion / 1 extra
carrot / 1 extra celery stalk /
1 fennel bulb / 2 tomatoes /
1 handful of button mushrooms

FOR FISH STOCK, ADD:

2 lb fish heads/bones (these can
be sourced from a fishmonger) /
1 fennel bulb

Depending on which stock you are making, you will need to adjust the amount of time
that you simmer your ingredients for:

- For chicken stock: 4–12 hours—the longer the better
- For beef stock: 4–12 hours—the longer the better
- For vegetable stock: 1–2 hours
- For fish stock: 1–2 hours
  NOTE: Do remember that if you're making beef stock, the beef bones need to be roasted
  for 45 minutes beforehand—don't forget to factor this into your preparation time.

1 / *Creamy, crunchy white sauce* **2 /** *Coconut-oil "hollandaise"* **3 /** *Walnut miso sauce*

4 / *Stir-fry sauce* **5 /** *Tangy herb sauce*

SAUCE

I believe a good sauce is key to a good dish. Throughout this book I have created lots of little extra sauces which upgrade simple dishes to meals bursting with flavor, but here are a few of my absolute favorites, which complement most foods: fish, meat, whatever you prefer.

CREAMY, CRUNCHY WHITE SAUCE

¾ cup coconut yogurt / 1½ tablespoons finely chopped shallots / 4 teaspoons finely chopped chives / 4 teaspoons finely chopped dill / 3 tablespoons finely chopped cucumber, skin on, seeds removed / 3 tablespoons fennel, finely chopped / 2 tablespoons lemon juice, plus some zest / 1 tablespoon olive oil / 1 level teaspoon sea salt flakes / ½ teaspoon toasted and crushed coriander seeds / lots of freshly ground black pepper

Simply mix all the ingredients together.

COCONUT-OIL "HOLLANDAISE"

4 egg yolks, preferably free-range or organic / ½ teaspoon Dijon mustard / ½ cup light vegetable or fish stock, or water / ½ teaspoon mild curry powder / 2 tablespoons melted coconut oil / 1 teaspoon lemon juice / zest of ½ a lemon

Heat a medium-size glass bowl over a saucepan of barely simmering water. Add the egg yolks, mustard, stock and curry powder to the bowl and whisk continuously over the heat for a few minutes, until the mixture starts to thicken.

Then slowly add the melted coconut oil and keep whisking until you have your "hollandaise" sauce. It should coat the back of a spoon and be of pouring consistency. Remove from the heat and whisk in the lemon juice and zest. This will slightly thicken the mixture further.

WALNUT MISO SAUCE

1 cup walnuts, halved / ½ cup chicken stock or water / 2 tablespoons miso /
1 tablespoon tahini / 1 tablespoon tamari / 1 tablespoon maple syrup

Roast the walnut halves in the oven at 350°F for 10 minutes, until warmed through and aromatic. Rub them in a tea towel to remove as much of the skin as possible, then place the nuts in a food processor. Add the rest of the ingredients and pulse to a smooth sauce.

STIR-FRY SAUCE

6 tablespoons coconut aminos / 4 tablespoons five spice powder / 1 teaspoon coconut syrup / 2 cloves of garlic / 1 deseeded chili / 1 teaspoon grated ginger

Put everything into a food processor and blend.

TANGY HERB SAUCE

2 tablespoons extra virgin olive oil / juice and zest of 1 lemon / ½ teaspoon apple cider vinegar / 1 teaspoon almond butter / a pinch of coconut sugar / freshly ground black pepper / 5 anchovy fillets, finely chopped / a small bunch (approx. 1 tablespoon) of fresh tarragon leaves, finely chopped / a small bunch (approx. 1 tablespoon) of fresh flat-leaf parsley, finely chopped / 1 clove of garlic, peeled and grated / sea salt

In a medium-size bowl, whisk together the oil, lemon juice and finely grated lemon zest (save some for garnishing), apple cider vinegar and almond butter until very smooth. Season with the coconut sugar and pepper. Add the anchovy fillets, along with the tarragon, flat-leaf parsley and garlic. Check if it needs salt, but the anchovies might be enough.

SALSA

Salsa (the Spanish word for sauce) is typically a tomato-based dip that originated in Mexico. Even though salsas are usually made primarily with chopped tomatoes, onions, chilies and bell peppers, they can also be made with fruits like mango and pineapple. They can range from very mild in flavor to incredibly hot, and the consistency can be smooth or coarse and chunky. Homemade salsa can be stored in a Mason jar for 5 to 7 days in the fridge or 1 to 2 months in the freezer (however, once thawed and/or opened, use within 2 to 3 days).

SALSA VERDE / MAKES ½ CUP

2 large handfuls of fresh parsley / 2 large handfuls of fresh cilantro /
2 large handfuls of fresh basil / 1 tablespoon capers / 1 x 2-ounce can of anchovies /
juice of ½ a lemon / 2 tablespoons extra virgin olive oil / sea salt and freshly
ground black pepper

First, finely chop all the herbs and put into a bowl (use a blender if you're pressed for time, but hand-cutting produces a fresher and more authentic result).

Finely chop the capers and anchovies, and add to the bowl. Add the lemon juice, and mix. Pour the olive oil in slowly, mixing as you go, until you reach a good consistency. Season with salt and pepper to taste.

Serve with grilled, poached or roasted fish or meat alongside green beans with a scattering of toasted almond flakes on top to add a bit of crunch (see opposite).

PERFECT PARTNER / *Salsa verde with halibut and green beans*

STAGE ONE / *Ingredients for Avocado papaya salsa*

"YOU DON'T HAVE TO EAT LESS. YOU JUST HAVE TO EAT RIGHT."

AVOCADO PAPAYA SALSA / SERVES 4

1 ripe papaya, or mango if unavailable / 1 firm avocado / ½ a small red onion /
1 red chili, deseeded / 1 large handful of basil / 1 large handful of cilantro /
1 lime, juiced and zested / juice of 1 lemon / a good pinch of salt / 1 teaspoon
raw honey (or other sweetener of your choice) / freshly ground black pepper

Peel and deseed the papaya and dice into small cubes. Do the same for the
avocado. Finely dice the onion and red chili, and put everything into a serving bowl.
Finely chop the herbs and add to the bowl, then add the lime zest and mix well.

Squeeze the lime and lemon juice into a jar, then add the salt and honey and mix
well. Pour this dressing over the salsa, combine well, season with a good pinch of
pepper and serve with white fish and chicken, or simply enjoy on its own.

STAGE TWO / *Deseed and dice*

STAGE THREE / *Ready to enjoy*

GUACAMOLE

Like salsa, guacamole also originated in Mexico and is used as a dip or a salad. It's traditionally made by mashing avocado with a little sea salt, garlic, lemon juice, olive oil and sometimes chopped tomato, chili and onion. It can be made smooth or chunky, with a blender or mortar and pestle. It's incredibly healthy thanks to the main ingredient, avocado, which is a good source of healthy fat, plus vitamins C, E and K and fiber. Like salsa, it can be stored for up to a week in the fridge and up to 2 months in a freezer, but once opened it should be used within a few days.

2 avocados, mashed / 1 small handful of spinach or kale, shredded / ¼ of a red onion, finely diced / juice of 1 lime / a good tablespoon of fresh, diced red chili (deseeded if you don't like heat) / 5 cherry tomatoes, chopped finely / 1 yellow pepper, diced finely / a generous handful of cilantro leaves, finely chopped / a pinch of cumin / a pinch of sea salt

Simply mix all the ingredients together in a bowl and enjoy! Serve with carrot sticks, crispy gem lettuce leaves or sweet potato chips.

HOMEMADE COCONUT BUTTER

This is a creamy, healthy alternative spread, which is incredibly easy to make and very versatile. It gives a richer texture than coconut oil and the butter will last for a few weeks unrefridgerated when properly sealed in a container or glass jar.

10 ounces dried, shredded or flaked coconut (unsweetened)

Put the coconut into the food processor and pulse. It will first get crumbly, then clumpy, but will slowly form a smooth paste as the oils in the coconut break down. The mixture will begin sticking to the sides of the food processor: keep pushing it down and pulsing until you have a smooth paste. Store in a clean jar. Spread on your favorite gluten-free toast—it'll all be gone before you know it!

FLAVORING IDEAS:

It's easy to add different flavors to coconut butter for use in cooking or as a spread:

Lemon zest/paprika/harissa: add as much as you like and spread on a cracker or piece of gluten-free bread; also good to cook with.

Raspberry/strawberry: blend one or two raspberries or strawberries and mix thoroughly into the finished coconut butter. Use as a light, coconutty jam.

Herbs: add finely chopped parsley, tarragon, basil, chives and salt to the finished butter, mix well, then keep in the fridge or freezer. Melt over grilled chicken or fish.

Chocolate: add a small amount of melted (minimum 70% cocoa) chocolate to the finished butter, mix well and allow to cool. Use as an alternative to chocolate spread.

HUMMUS

Originally an Egyptian dish, hummus's main ingredient is chickpeas, which are mashed with tahini, olive oil, garlic, salt and lemon juice. However, you can get far more creative with it and use the base as a great way to eat a wider variety of vegetables.

PUY LENTIL HUMMUS

½ cup Puy lentils /sea salt and freshly ground black pepper / 1 clove of garlic / 2 tablespoons extra virgin olive oil / juice of ½ a lemon / 2 teaspoons ground cumin, toasted / 1–2 teaspoons white tahini / 2 tablespoons hazelnut butter

Bring 1–1¼ cup water to a simmer in a medium saucepan and cook the lentils for 20 to 25 minutes until tender, over low heat. Add salt, to taste, at the end and set aside for 5 minutes. Then drain, reserving any cooking water.

Put the cooked lentils into a Vitamix or heavy-duty food processor with the rest of the ingredients and blend until smooth. If the mixture seems a little dry, add some of the reserved cooking water (approximately 4 tablespoons) until you reach your desired consistency. Add salt and pepper to taste.

Serve with crudités such as cucumber, carrot, mixed pepper and zucchini sticks, radishes, broccoli florets and rye or toasted sourdough bread.

Note: You could also use green or red lentils if you like.

GREEN HUMMUS

1 x 13.5-ounce can of chickpeas in water, drained and rinsed well / 3 tablespoons tahini / 1 clove of garlic / a handful (approx. 2 tablespoons) of fresh spinach, roughly chopped / 12 fresh basil leaves / 1 avocado, halved, peeled and pit removed, roughly chopped / 4 tablespoons olive oil / 2 lemons, juiced / 1 small lemon, zested / 1 teaspoon fine sea salt / freshly ground black pepper

Blend all the ingredients together in a food processor until smooth and creamy. This hummus can be stored in a glass jar in the fridge for up to 3 days. Serve with salad, vegetable crudités, on gluten-free crackers or bread, or with fish or chicken.

GREEN HARISSA

This is a Tunisian hot chili paste made with red peppers, serrano peppers and any other hot chili peppers you fancy, plus garlic, coriander seeds and olive oil. I love it and it's something I use in my kitchen all the time. If truth be told, you can buy some very good harissa in the shops, but many are filled with a lot of nonsense, so if you do buy yours ready-made, always check the labels and try to buy a good-quality one. However, it's far cheaper, healthier and more fun to make your own. It lasts for ages in the fridge (you can freeze it too—it works very well in ice cube trays) and all you need is a dollop added to any dish to turn it from bland to having a blast of flavor (you can go as hot as you dare!). Some food markets sell dried-herb harissa mixes, which are also a great addition to your store cupboard. I put this on top of almost any dish at any time of day. I love it!

2 tablespoons cumin seeds, toasted / 1 tablespoon coriander seeds, toasted /
2 green chilies, roughly chopped and seeds removed / 1 shallot, sliced /
1 clove of garlic, peeled and roughly chopped / ½ cup extra virgin olive oil /
1 bunch of fresh flat-leaf parsley, stems removed / 1 bunch of fresh cilantro,
stems removed / zest and juice of 1 lemon / a good pinch of sea salt

Blend all the ingredients together in a food processor, keeping a little bit of texture. This paste can be kept in a glass jar in the fridge for up to 3 days and is great to serve with fish, chicken, beans, eggs or veggies.

TAPENADE

Tapenade is a rich, rough-textured paste made of olives and olive oil mixed with capers and anchovies, and often other flavors such as lemon, garlic, mustard, basil or parsley. The paste is hugely popular in France and Italy, where it is usually served as an appetizer spread on bread, or stuffed in meats or on fish. It is worth using stone-in olives in this recipe if you have the time to pit them yourself—the flavor is considerably better.

5 ounces Kalamata olives (pitted weight) / 2 tablespoons capers /
3 anchovy fillets / juice and zest of ½ a lemon / 1 sprig of fresh thyme,
leaves picked / a small handful of fresh parsley / 1 clove of garlic /
1 tablespoon extra virgin olive oil

Blend all the ingredients—apart from the oil—together in a food processor. Transfer to a bowl, add the extra virgin olive oil and mix in thoroughly using a spoon, until the mixture comes together like a paste.

"A HEALTHY OUTSIDE STARTS FROM THE INSIDE."

KALE AND ALMOND PESTO

The traditional ingredients for a pesto recipe (originally from northern Italy) are basil, Parmesan cheese, pine nuts, garlic, lemon and olive oil, which are mixed together either using a mortar and pestle or a blender until you get a smooth, slightly granular texture. To keep my pesto dairy-free, I leave out the Parmesan and I replace the pine nuts with other types for variety. I also like to use different vegetables and herbs.

A favorite of mine is pesto made with kale and almonds; sometimes I'll add sun-dried tomatoes and chili, or cilantro and cashew nuts. So get creative! Take a recipe and play around with it according to your tastes and dietary requirements. You can then add pesto to your salads, fish or meat, or stir it into your spiralized vegetables for a lovely, comforting "pasta" dish. Pesto is something I always have in the fridge because it's so simple to make and livens up every meal. It lasts up to 6 months in the freezer and a week in the fridge (even after it's been opened). Add a layer of olive oil on top to help keep it fresh.

1 bunch of basil leaves / 1 lemon, juiced and zested / ½ cup olive oil / 1 clove of garlic / 4 ounces soaked almonds, drained / ¼ pound kale, washed and roughly chopped / sea salt

Blend all the ingredients together, keeping the mixture slightly chunky. Add sea salt to taste. Check the flavor and adjust as you prefer—you might like a touch more garlic, lemon or basil.

DRESSING

Most store-bought salad dressings, including the seemingly healthy or "low fat" ones, are full of sugar and/or salt, and sometimes other unnecessary fillers such as corn starch, and are occasionally made with the less healthy vegetable oils. The low-fat ones in particular are best avoided because they actually prevent your body from absorbing certain antioxidants (including carotenoids, which are found in yellow, red and orange vegetables) in your salad. One study from Purdue University found that having certain fats in your dressing, like olive oil, helps your body fully absorb the health benefits from your salad.[1] So ignore the fat-free labels and make your own dressings. And remember, every salad needs a little natural fat in it so that you can absorb all its goodness. This is because some vitamins are fat-soluble and you need a little bit of fat so your body can absorb nutrients.

MUSTARD DRESSING

1 cup olive oil / 1 teaspoon mustard powder / ½ cup apple cider vinegar / sea salt and freshly ground black pepper, to taste

Simply mix all the ingredients together. If you find you need a little sweetness, add a dash of fresh apple juice or some coconut sugar, but it's best to get used to eating without the need to sweeten.

LEMON AND GARLIC DRESSING

1 cup olive oil / 1 garlic clove, crushed / ½ a chili (deseeded if you don't like too much spice) / juice of 1 lemon

Get creative and don't use only olive oil. Try nut oils in this one such as hazelnut, walnut or macadamia. And avocado oil has a wonderful flavor. Simply mix all the ingredients together.

---

1. http://www.purdue.edu/newsroom/research/2012/120619FerruzziSalad.html

FROZEN HERB AND SPICE MIXES

These are really useful to have in your freezer to throw over vegetables or proteins when you're steam-frying or sautéing them. I'm a huge fan of using herbs this way because it's so simple. I used to buy herbs, then forget to water them and they'd dry out, or I'd buy packages of herbs and they would go bad within a few days, before I'd had a chance to use them all. So now I just pop all the ingredients into a blender, or use a handheld blender with a beaker attachment, and roughly chop everything together. Then I freeze them so they're ready to be used in cooking whenever I need them. Just a quick tip: you don't want to chop the herbs so finely that they turn into a mushy paste—keep the texture a bit rough. Here are a few frozen herb combinations I love but, as ever, I urge you to get creative and make up your own mixes:

◆ Chili, garlic, lemongrass, ginger and cilantro
◆ Basil, oregano, garlic and shallot
◆ Chili, cumin seeds and coriander seeds
◆ Fresh turmeric root, lemon zest and chili
◆ Mushroom, tarragon, shallot and lemon zest

FROZEN HERBS IN OIL

This is a great way to preserve your herbs and add a really quick pop of flavor to roasts, stews, soups or vegetables.

Use fresh herbs such as thyme, rosemary, oregano or sage. Put a small amount of one or a mixture of herbs into each ice cube tray. You can keep them whole or roughly chop, it's up to you. I do both. Pour olive oil or melted coconut butter over each and freeze overnight, then remove them from the trays and put into bags to use when making winter stews, soups, roasts or when sautéing vegetables.

Citrus zest, grated ginger and fresh chili also work really well, so get creative and make up some interesting mixes. Just remember to label the bags. You can also use melted butter or ghee if you aren't sensitive to these.

FLAVORED OIL

You can also add fresh herbs to oil to create a flavored oil to add directly to food. The shelf life isn't very long though, so make it in small quantities. Get an old glass water bottle or olive oil bottle and fill halfway with olive oil, then add your herbs and let them infuse. I love to use tarragon with chili and garlic, or rosemary and garlic. Have a play around. They look so pretty and really can add a lovely punch of flavor to your food.

Here are my favorite flavor combinations I love to make up when I have leftover herbs:

- Tarragon, chili and garlic
- Rosemary and garlic
- Chili and cumin seeds
- Lemon and mint

FERMENTED FOOD

As I was writing this book fermented foods were really taking off and now they're all the rage. I'm so glad, because as well as adding fantastic flavor to your meals they're also incredibly healthy, particularly for your gut, which we now know impacts overall health. In fact, some experts believe that nearly all the health problems in the body relate back to the gut in some way, and that a healthy gut can help to reduce your risk of certain cancers, heart disease, depression, skin conditions like eczema and acne, and improve your immunity. This is why fermented foods are so good for us. The fermentation process creates a rich source of probiotics and prebiotics that are beneficial to the flora in our digestive tract (the process also makes these foods great sources of B vitamins). Eating small amounts of fermented foods every day is great for healthy gut bacteria because as we digest them, they break down in a way that introduces healthy bacteria into the gut.

Fermented foods, like apple cider vinegar, sauerkraut, fermented cabbage, miso soup, kefir (a fermented milk drink) and kombucha tea can be found in most good supermarkets and all health food stores. My favorite fermented food is kimchi which is a delicious Korean dish of fermented cabbage. I urge you to give it a try even though it may not sound appetizing—it packs a flavor punch and tastes amazing.

KIMCHI / MAKES APPROX. 2–3 QUARTS

2 Chinese cabbages / 2 tablespoons coarse sea salt / 4 spring onions, thinly sliced

For the seasoning paste: optional: 2 tablespoons salted shrimp / ¼ cup fish sauce / ½ cup gelatinous beef stock / 1 bulb of garlic, cloves peeled and minced / 1 teaspoon finely grated fresh ginger (approx. 1 ounce) / 2 teaspoons maple syrup (or other sweetener of your choice) / 2 tablespoons ground cayenne / 1 piece of kombu / ¾ ounce chili flakes

Cut the cabbage into quarters and then cut each piece in half lengthwise, removing the core. Lay each cabbage segment flat, then cut into sections about ¾ inch wide by 4 inches long. Cut any larger leaves down to approximately this size. In a big bowl, toss the cabbage with the salt and set aside for 1 hour and 15 minutes. Rinse off the salt in a bowl of cold water and let the cabbage leaves drain in a colander for 20 minutes.

To make the seasoning paste, purée the shrimp (if using), fish sauce, beef stock, garlic, ginger, maple syrup, cayenne and kombu in a small food processor. Transfer the mixture to a bowl and mix in the chili flakes. Let the seasoning paste sit for 15 minutes to allow the flavors to combine.

In a large bowl, toss the cabbage and spring onions with the spicy paste and mix until evenly distributed. Pack tightly into a 2- or 3-quart container, cover and set aside for 2 days at room temperature. Then move the container to a refrigerator. The chilled kimchi will keep for up to 2 weeks.

Chapter 3

EATING THE RAINBOW

Chapter 3 /
EATING THE RAINBOW

———————

Raw kale salad with ginger dressing

Sweet potato cakes with grilled tiger shrimp
and ginger-saffron yogurt

Asian chicken salad

Mediterranean "pasta"

Herby green bread

Smoked mackerel lettuce boats

Chicken breast with ginger
and apricot stuffing

Halibut ceviche

Colorful layered eggs

Green "wake me up" broth

Beet soup

Mussels four ways:
Mussels Provençale / Mussels with white wine, fennel
and tarragon / Fragrant coconut milk mussels /
Asian-style mussels

Growing up, we were told to eat our greens, but this was only partly right. While green vegetables are a powerhouse of healthful properties, having the other colors in our diet is just as important. Brightly colored foods contain naturally occurring phytochemicals, which are responsible for giving food its color—the fire-engine red of tomatoes; the deep purple hue of blueberries—and also play important roles in protecting our health and staving off chronic disease: mopping up inflammation, slowing down premature aging, supporting sight, protecting the brain and assisting our immune system. Yet for many of us, the color beige is the mainstay of our plates. Foods like cereal, pasta, rice, pastries, chicken and bread often dominate our meals. These foods, especially when processed or bleached, offer much lower levels and less variety of nutrients than we need to keep healthy. I'm not saying don't eat them, but I am saying aim for the rainbow when it comes to your daily food choices.

Research has shown that our diets should be predominantly plant-based, and so ensuring that we include plant foods in each meal is an important habit to embrace. Every cell in our body survives on the nutrients it is fed—plant foods are the richest sources of vitamins, minerals, fiber and those color-giving phytonutrients, which form their own cool little health-defending gang.

When humans were predominantly hunter-gatherers we ate over 800 different varieties of plant foods. These days we have a very limited choice, especially when shopping in supermarkets. But at farmers' markets you'll find the more unusual forms of our everyday foods, such as purple carrots, golden beets, yellow zucchini, orange tomatoes and purple broccoli—there really is a wider variety out there to shake us out of our color comfort zone.

Many experts advise us to eat five portions of fruits and vegetables per day, but they don't stipulate that they need to be in a natural, unprocessed form. And I believe that we really need much, much more. I encourage you to eat three portions of fruit per day, one per meal (a portion being a small handful), and two to three portions of vegetables at each meal, reaching as far and wide in color as possible.

As you go through your day, try to mentally tick off the different colors you are eating. And see where you could possibly add in an extra burst. For example, a salad doesn't have to be only lettuce, cucumber, tomato and a dressing. Throw in some other dark leafy greens like spinach, broccoli, brightly colored peppers, red cabbage, carrots, beets and creamy green avocado too. If you're making oatmeal for breakfast, toss in some fresh berries or make a smoothie with one fruit and three or four different vegetables. It's easy once you start.

And while on the subject of plant foods, wherever possible try to buy local, in season and organic produce so that your plants are as unadulterated as possible, which means more nutrients and the best flavor.

As a general rule, the darker, deeper or brighter the color the more nutrients the food contains. The four main color groups to aim for are red, green, purple/blue and orange/yellow—try to get a good mix of these throughout the day.

So here's how to de-beige your diet . . .

PICK SOMETHING RED

Like what? Tomatoes, raspberries, strawberries, red or pink apples, rhubarb, red grapes, watermelons, radishes, cranberries, beets, guava, cherries, pomegranates, pink grapefruit, chilies and red bell peppers.

Why? Red or pink foods are rich in vitamin C. A lot of them (tomatoes, peppers, watermelons and pink grapefruit) contain lycopene, a powerful health-boosting antioxidant which has been shown to help protect against certain cancers. There are hugely exciting scientific advances occurring at the moment that are revealing the full transformative impact eating well can have on your health. One study[1]—from Harvard Medical School—found that men with a lycopene-rich diet can reduce their risk of prostate cancer by 35 percent. As a nutritional therapist, these studies bring me such joy because it's wonderful to see the results of a healthy diet locked down in science. Studies also show that our bodies absorb lycopene more effectively when the food has been heated, so roasted tomatoes are healthier than raw ones (although raw ones are still incredibly good for us). Healthy fats, like coconut oil or olive oil, for example, enhance the absorption of lycopene even further. So roasted cherry tomatoes drizzled with a little olive oil will pack a real nutritional punch.

---

1. Abstract to prostate cancer study: http://www.ncbi.nlm.nih.gov/pubmed/12424325

Then there's anthocyanins, pigments which give red fruits and vegetables their color. Studies show they can help to reduce our risk of cancer, improve heart health and vision, reduce your risk of strokes, improve brain function and prevent urinary tract infections.

PICK SOMETHING GREEN

Like what? Where do I begin? There are so many greens to choose from, including spinach, kale, arugula, lettuce, asparagus, leeks, avocados, watercress, cucumbers, zucchini, broccoli, green peppers, green beans, green apples, kiwi fruit, green grapes, Brussels sprouts, cabbages, sugar snap peas and celery. Plus herbs like mint, parsley, tarragon and basil.

Why? Naturally green foods contain chlorophyll, the pigment found in dark green vegetables and algae, which gives them their color. The health benefits of chlorophyll are said to include replenishing red blood cells which can improve energy, increasing blood flow and oxygen in blood and improving digestion, and studies have even suggested it can help reduce cancer risk.

Green foods are also full of folate, vitamin K, potassium, iron, calcium and beta-carotene and contain the nutrients lutein and zeaxanthin, which studies suggest can help to improve eye health and reduce age-related macular degeneration (which can eventually lead to blindness).

PICK SOMETHING PURPLE/BLUE

Like what? Blueberries, blackberries, blackcurrants, plums, prunes, red onions, red cabbage, eggplant, purple grapes and purple cauliflower.

Why? Like some red fruits, purple and deep-blue foods are colored by the phytochemicals anthocyanins. One study[2] found that blueberries—considered to have one of the highest antioxidant contents of all fruits and vegetables—may slow down breast cancer cell growth.

And resveratrol, found mainly in black grapes, "mops up" potentially harmful and aging free radicals in the environment and can help to reduce inflammation in the body and slow the aging process.

---

2. This blueberry/breast cancer study is from the Beckman Research Institute, City of Hope: http://www.cityofhope.org/superfoods#Blueberries

PICK SOMETHING ORANGE/YELLOW

Like what? Pumpkins, apricots, all types of melons, peaches, sweet potatoes, carrots, yellow and orange peppers, grapefruit, mangoes, papayas, turnips, nectarines, sweet corn, satsumas, oranges, bananas and butternut squash. Plus spices like turmeric.

Why? Yellow and orange foods are a great source of vitamin C, plus they often contain beta-carotene, converted by the body to vitamin A, which can help improve digestive health and vision. Some orange and yellow foods (mangoes, peaches, peppers, nectarines and citrus fruits, for example) also contain beta-cryptoxanthin, which can help to protect respiratory health and improve bone growth, vision and immunity. Like lycopene, these types of carotenoids are absorbed more efficiently when eaten with fat, so roast some squash with coconut oil or sprinkle a few nuts over your melon.

Pineapple is a good source of bromelain, which is a digestive-boosting enzyme, and citrus fruits have been shown to protect against breast and skin cancer.

Last, but by no means least, there's turmeric, one of my absolute favorite ingredients to cook with. I have a large jar of this in my kitchen because I love to add it to lots of different dishes. This bright-yellow spice has anti-inflammatory properties, which can help brain function, immunity and digestive health, and it's fantastic for warding off seasonal coughs and colds.

I don't encourage any kind of obsessions around food, be it counting calories or weighing protein portions—and that also goes for colors. Don't get hung up on it, just observe the colors on your plate each day, and when shopping try to pick up fruits and vegetables that you haven't tried before and to extend your variety of colors. That's all I ask—because the food we eat can quickly, quietly and powerfully make great changes to our health.

While the whole of this book contains colorful, natural, health-promoting foods, this chapter specifically focuses on recipes that are rich sources of phytonutrients to help you upgrade your meals and not only find the rainbow, but the pot of gold too!

RAW KALE SALAD WITH GINGER DRESSING

All hail the kale! If you haven't been juicing it or blending it for the last year, where have you been? I wanted to include this salad in the book to show you how to make kale tasty, so you can eat it in its solid form rather than blending it all the time. Again, this is something I make a lot of so that I can then add it to other salads. I particularly love it served with this ginger dressing. However, despite kale being the trendiest kid on the block, it's not something you should be eating in abundance—particularly if you have a thyroid condition—so go steady with it.

INGREDIENTS

¼ pound kale
1 teaspoon sea salt
1 orange, peeled and cut into segments
1 small red onion, peeled and finely diced
1 avocado, peeled and cut into cubes
optional: a squeeze of orange juice and a
   handful of seeds to serve

For the dressing:
1 teaspoon raw ginger juice
   (finely grating a ¾-inch piece of fresh
   ginger, then squeezing it through a
   cloth, will extract approximately this
   quantity of ginger juice)
2 teaspoons raw honey
3 tablespoons macadamia nut oil
2 tablespoons raw apple cider vinegar
1 teaspoon Dijon mustard
juice of ½ a lemon

Remove the stems from the kale leaves and cut them into strips. Combine with the salt in a large bowl and massage. Put a weight, like a plate with a bottle of water on top of it, on it and wait for 15 minutes. Toss the kale again and replace the weight for a further 10 to 15 minutes. Drain and rinse thoroughly in several changes of water. Spin dry.

To make the dressing, blend all the ingredients in a Vitamix or food processor.

Combine the orange, onion and avocado with the kale. Add a squeeze of orange juice and a handful of seeds, if you like. Pour the dressing over and serve.

SWEET POTATO CAKES WITH GRILLED TIGER SHRIMP AND GINGER-SAFFRON YOGURT

I love a sweet potato cake. When I came up with this recipe, I was thinking along the lines of potato croquettes, as they are such a comforting food. Sweet potatoes have a great color and they are more nutritious than white potatoes. Go easy on them if you're looking to lose weight though.

This recipe is lovely to have as a treat meal or if you are entertaining, as it's super easy to make. Once you've got the hang of the sweet potato cakes, try using other combinations of ingredients, like broccoli and spinach, to make a patty with this method, or simply combine potato and fish to make a fishcake.

INGREDIENTS

3 medium-sized sweet potatoes, peeled (approx. 1¾ pounds)
1 egg, preferably free-range or organic
3 tablespoons coconut flour
3 spring onions, chopped
1 teaspoon sea salt
freshly ground black pepper
coconut oil
16 raw tiger shrimp, peeled and deveined

For the ginger-saffron yogurt:
a pinch of saffron threads
½ cup coconut yogurt
1 teaspoon finely grated fresh ginger
1 tablespoon extra virgin olive oil
sea salt and freshly ground black pepper
a squeeze of lemon juice
optional: a tablespoon each of freshly chopped cilantro and mint

Steam or boil your sweet potatoes for 10 to 12 minutes until soft. Drain and dry the potatoes in the pan for 1 to 2 minutes, then mash them until smooth. Mix in the egg, coconut flour, spring onions, salt and pepper. Form 12 lime-sized balls and press these into patties, about ½ inch thick. If making ahead, chill the cakes in the fridge until you are ready to cook them.

Add ½ tablespoon of boiling water to the saffron threads and leave to cool. Remove from the water and mix them into the coconut yogurt with the ginger, olive oil, salt and pepper. Squeeze in a little lemon juice. You can add cilantro and mint as well, if you wish.

Put 2 tablespoons of coconut oil into a large non-stick frying pan over medium heat. Fry the cakes for 3 to 4 minutes on each side, until golden brown.

Quickly sauté the shrimp in a non-stick pan in a little coconut oil for 2 minutes on each side, until pink and cooked through. Serve the patties with a dollop of ginger-saffron yogurt over the top and the shrimp on the side.

ASIAN CHICKEN SALAD

I think a salad should never feel like a miserable meal, and Asian flavors are a wonderful way to give life to a simple dish. Here is a salad that has been a staple in my life for many years.

INGREDIENTS

For the chicken:
2 x 5-ounce chicken breasts
2 stalks of lemongrass, bruised
4 sprigs of fresh cilantro
a thumb-sized piece of fresh ginger, sliced
2 cloves of garlic, smashed
2 red or green chilies, cut in half
  lengthwise (deseeded if you like)
sea salt

For the salad:
1 small papaya or mango, peeled,
  seeds removed and cut into
  ½-inch slices
¼ of a white or red cabbage, finely
  shredded (I use a mandolin)
1 small carrot, washed and cut into
  ribbons using a peeler
½ a cucumber, cut into ribbons using
  a peeler

For the dressing:
6 tablespoons extra virgin olive oil
2 tablespoons apple cider vinegar
juice of 1 lime
sea salt and freshly ground black pepper

To garnish:
1 red chili, sliced
a handful of crushed cashew nuts
a handful of fresh cilantro leaves

First, prepare the chicken. Put the chicken breasts into a pan and cover with cold water. Add the lemongrass, cilantro sprigs, ginger slices, garlic cloves, chilies and a good pinch of salt. Bring to a simmer, switch off the heat and immediately cover the pan with a lid. Allow the chicken to sit in the hot poaching liquor for 20 minutes. Once cooked, remove from the pan and allow to cool (discard the poaching liquor). Shred the chicken into fine strips.

Put the papaya or mango slices, shredded cabbage, carrot and cucumber into a large bowl. Add the shredded chicken.

To make the dressing, whisk the olive oil, vinegar, lime juice and seasoning together. Pour the dressing over the salad in the bowl and toss.

Divide the salad between two plates and serve with the garnishes.

"EAT FOOD.
NOT TOO MUCH.
MOSTLY PLANTS."

MICHAEL POLLAN

MEDITERRANEAN "PASTA"

This is the ideal quick bowl of comfort food. It came about when I was hunting in a sparsely stocked fridge after a long day, when all I really wanted was a delicious garlicky bowl of pasta! However, I managed to resist and quickly spiralized a lovely fat yellow zucchini that I had from my garden. Thank goodness for some cherry tomatoes, a jar of olives, a couple of cloves of garlic, the zest of a lemon, basil and a bit of olive oil—*voilà!* For a little hit of heat, add some dried chili flakes.

INGREDIENTS

olive oil
2 cloves of garlic, peeled and finely
   chopped
1 large green or yellow zucchini, spiralized
a handful of cherry tomatoes, quartered
a handful of black olives
a pinch of dried chili flakes
zest of ½ a lemon
a few fresh basil leaves

Put a drizzle of olive oil and the garlic into a pan and place on a medium heat. Add the zucchini noodles and sauté so they heat through and start to color. Toss in the cherry tomatoes, black olives and chili flakes and mix together. Before serving, sprinkle with the lemon zest and tear the basil leaves over top.

HERBY GREEN BREAD

This delicious green bread is more cakey than bready in texture, because it's gluten free. It's really nice toasted for breakfast with a poached egg, but as it will fall apart quite easily (because of the lack of gluten), it won't toast very well in a toaster. Instead, put it on a baking sheet under the broiler. The bread will last for about 3 days, if you haven't eaten it all by then!

INGREDIENTS

4½ tablespoons coconut butter, plus extra
   for greasing, see page 71
1¾ cups almond flour, plus extra for dusting
a pinch of sea salt
1½ teaspoons baking powder
¼ teaspoon baking soda
1 large bunch of kale
1 zucchini
1 clove of garlic, peeled
fresh herbs: basil, chives and parsley,
   1 large handful of each
3 eggs, preferably free-range or organic,
   beaten
3 tablespoons coconut milk
1 teaspoon lemon juice
1 tablespoon apple cider vinegar

Preheat the oven to 350°F. Grease and flour an 8-inch x 4-inch loaf pan using a little coconut butter and a dusting of almond flour.

In a large bowl, combine the almond flour, salt, baking powder and baking soda. Pulse the kale, zucchini, garlic and herbs in a food processor, or chop it all finely, and add to the bowl along with the eggs, coconut milk, lemon juice, coconut butter and apple cider vinegar. Mix well.

Spoon the mixture into the prepared loaf pan and flatten the surface using the back of a spoon dipped in cold water. Bake the loaf on the middle rack of the oven for 45 minutes, or until an inserted metal skewer comes out clean. Turn out onto a wire rack to cool before serving.

SMOKED MACKEREL LETTUCE BOATS

Smoked mackerel is widely available in most supermarkets and is an excellent source of healthy fats. I love to wrap it in these lettuce leaves to make my version of a sandwich, and the addition of avocado, another source of healthy fats, will ensure that you'll feel nicely full.

INGREDIENTS

2 spring onions, finely chopped
8 cherry tomatoes, cut into quarters
1 avocado, peeled, pitted and chopped
1 small eating apple, cored and
   finely chopped or grated
a squeeze of lemon juice
sea salt and freshly ground
   black pepper
4 smoked mackerel fillets, flaked
optional: ¼ teaspoon freshly
   grated horseradish
1 gem lettuce
a small handful of fresh cilantro,
   chopped

First, make the filling: mix the spring onions, cherry tomatoes, avocado, apple, lemon juice and seasoning together in a large bowl. Add the flaked mackerel and horseradish (if using) and fold in gently.

Separate the lettuce leaves and arrange on a serving board or plate. Spoon the mackerel filling inside and sprinkle with the chopped cilantro to serve.

CHICKEN BREAST WITH GINGER AND APRICOT STUFFING

This is one of my favorite dishes—it's absolutely delicious. I urge anyone who thinks chicken is boring to try this recipe.

INGREDIENTS

coconut oil
1 banana shallot, peeled and
    finely chopped
1 clove of garlic, peeled and
    finely grated
1 teaspoon finely grated fresh ginger
2.5 ounces dried unsulphured apricots,
    finely chopped
3 tablespoons cashew nuts, soaked
    in water for 1 hour, drained and
    roughly chopped
2 tablespoons chopped fresh flat-leaf
    parsley
sea salt and freshly ground black pepper
2 x 5-ounce skinless chicken breasts

Preheat the oven to 350°F.

Heat a medium non-stick frying pan over medium heat and add 2 tablespoons of coconut oil. Add the shallot, garlic and ginger and sauté for 2 to 3 minutes to soften. Stir in the chopped apricots, cashew nuts and parsley and cook for another minute. Season to taste with salt and pepper. Remove from the heat and allow to cool.

Using a small sharp knife, cut along the side of each chicken breast to make a pocket, making sure you don't cut all the way through. Once the ginger and apricot mixture has cooled, divide it evenly between the chicken breasts, spooning it into the pockets. Press together and use toothpicks (three per breast) to secure the seam.

Transfer the chicken breasts to a non-stick baking pan and roast in the oven for 25 to 30 minutes, until golden brown and cooked through. Serve with the juices from the pan poured over and a simple green salad.

HALIBUT CEVICHE

I was really excited when I came up with this dish. I love to eat ceviche when on holiday and it just happened that I had some fresh halibut so thought I'd give it a try. Thank goodness it worked—it's totally delicious. Feel free to play around with different varieties of fish—haddock or pollock, for example.

INGREDIENTS

¼ cup lemon juice
¼ cup lime juice
¼ cup orange juice
1 large fresh red chili, deseeded and finely chopped
1 pound ultra-fresh halibut fillet
2 tablespoons finely chopped red or yellow deseeded pepper
2 tablespoons finely chopped, peeled and deseeded cucumber
1 avocado, chopped
2 tablespoons finely chopped fresh cilantro
2 teaspoons finely chopped fresh chives
1 tablespoon extra virgin olive oil
2 teaspoons maple syrup
sea salt and freshly ground black pepper
1 gem lettuce, to serve

Blend the citrus juices together and add the chopped chili.

Cut the fish into thin strips and put into a large bowl with the citrus juices and chili, so that the fish is completely covered (top up with more lemon or lime juice if you need to). Cover and leave to rest in the fridge for 2 hours.

Drain (and discard) the juices from the fish and transfer the fish to a serving platter. Mix the pepper, cucumber, avocado, cilantro and chives in a bowl. Mix in the olive oil and the maple syrup and season to taste with salt and pepper. Spoon the dressing over the fish and serve with crunchy leaves of gem lettuce.

COLORFUL LAYERED EGGS

While an omelet can be a very quick and easy staple, it can also, in fact, be an exquisitely simple, satisfying meal for any time of day. Julia Child gave the humble omelet eight pages in her book *Mastering the Art of French Cooking*, and chefs in France are hired on the basis of how well they make an omelet. The idea being that if they can't make one with flair and expertise, they won't have skill enough to make anything else!

INGREDIENTS

For the tomato-saffron layer:
2 medium vine tomatoes, scored, blanched
  and skinned
olive oil
a pinch of saffron threads
2 eggs, preferably free-range or organic,
  beaten
sea salt and freshly ground black pepper

For the tapenade layer:
⅛ cup black-olive tapenade
2 eggs, preferably free-range or organic,
  beaten

For the herb layer:
2 stalks each of basil, parsley and
  tarragon
2 tablespoons chive stalks
2 eggs, preferably free-range or organic,
  beaten
sea salt and freshly ground black pepper

To make the tomato-saffron mixture, chop the tomatoes once they are cool enough to handle. Heat a drizzle of oil in a pan and cook the tomatoes with the saffron for 2 minutes. Leave to cool, then blend with the beaten eggs and seasoning. For the tapanade layer, simply blend the tapenade with the beaten eggs. Then make the herb layer. Chop the herbs and chives, mix into the eggs and add seasoning.

When your three mixtures are ready, heat a small non-stick frying pan (approx. 8-inch). When hot, add a little olive oil and fry a thin layer of the tomato-saffron mixture on just one side until it has set. Set aside on a plate, add a little more olive oil to the pan and repeat with the tapenade mixture. When it's done, remove it from the pan and place it on top of the tomato-saffron omelet. Repeat with a touch more oil and the herb mixture and place this omelet on top of the other layers.

Start again with the tomato-saffron mixture and repeat until you have no more mixture left. Cover the layered omelet with parchment paper and weigh it down with a plate and a heavy object on top, such as a couple of cans. Leave to cool in the fridge overnight, then slice off the edges to neaten it up and cut into cubes or rectangles. Lovely with a salad, and perfect food for when you're on the go.

GREEN "WAKE ME UP" BROTH

Many of my clients recoil at the thought of vegetables at breakfast. But once you get over the idea and change your preconceptions about breakfast foods, this really is a beautiful way to start the day. However, you could drink this broth at any time to give you a lovely, natural burst of energy—best not before bed, though!

INGREDIENTS

sea salt
¼ pound leeks, white part only, finely chopped
¼ pound baby spinach
4 spears of green asparagus
3½ cups chicken stock (see pages 58–9)
1 piece of kombu seaweed, approx. 0.7 ounce (some kombu comes in sheets, so cut off the amount you need)
1 teaspoon matcha green tea powder
½ cup fresh or frozen baby peas
1 Granny Smith apple, skin on, cored and chopped into small cubes

Bring a big pot of water to a boil and add a generous pinch of sea salt. Blanch the chopped leeks for 7 minutes and refresh in ice-cold water. Then blanch the spinach and asparagus for 1 minute each and refresh in ice-cold water.

Heat the stock with the kombu seaweed. Once it is simmering, take a few tablespoons of stock out and add it to a bowl with the matcha tea, little by little, while stirring. First you'll have a thick paste, then add more stock until you have a runny mixture.

Add the peas to the pan of stock and heat for another 2 minutes, then add the leeks, spinach, asparagus, chopped apple and the blended matcha tea. Discard the kombu. Remove the pan from the heat, stir and serve.

BEET SOUP

This is a really pure soup, unlike so many store-bought ones. Make a large batch and store it in portions in the freezer for busy days. You don't need to serve anything else alongside—it's nutritionally complete just as it is.

INGREDIENTS

olive oil
1 onion, chopped
2 cloves of garlic, finely chopped
¾ pound fresh tomatoes, chopped
1 pound beets, cubed (the pre-cooked, vacuum-packed beet that's most common in supermarkets is okay, but make sure it's not with added vinegar)
2 cups chicken stock
sea salt and freshly ground black pepper
optional: coconut cream, fresh dill and chopped walnuts, to serve

Heat 1 tablespoon of olive oil in a large saucepan and gently sweat the onion until translucent. Add the garlic and tomatoes, stir well and cook for a further 5 minutes.

Add the beets, then pour the stock over until the vegetables are just covered, adding extra water if needed. Bring to a boil, then reduce the heat and simmer gently for 10 minutes.

Blend with an immersion blender until smooth—the soup should be a glorious purple.

Serve drizzled with coconut cream and topped with fresh dill and walnuts.

"I HAVE DECIDED
TO BE HAPPY
BECAUSE IT'S GOOD
FOR MY HEALTH."

MUSSELS FOUR WAYS

Mussels are such a quick and easy thing to cook for dinner. The thing I love about them is that they can be flavored in so many different ways. I've therefore given you four different flavor-choices, from a garlic and fennel option to a French tomato-based sauce; or you can opt for the more Asian-inspired base which is flavored with coconut aminos in place of soy. I adore the fragrant coconut version in the photograph (see page 119).

MUSSELS PROVENÇALE

INGREDIENTS

coconut oil
2 cloves of garlic, crushed
1 large red onion, finely chopped
8 sprigs of fresh thyme, leaves picked,
   plus 2 more, to serve
1 glass (approx. 6 ounces) dry white wine
1 x 13.5-ounce can of chopped tomatoes
2 pounds mussels, cleaned and debearded
juice of 1 lemon
4 tablespoons capers
freshly ground black pepper

Heat 1 tablespoon coconut oil in a wok or medium-size saucepan with a lid. Add the garlic, red onion and thyme and fry for 3 to 4 minutes. Add the wine, let it sizzle for 30 seconds, then add the canned tomatoes and simmer for 20 minutes. Throw in the mussels, place the lid on the pan and steam for 3 minutes. Give the pan a shake, remove the lid and stir. Discard any mussels that remain closed. Add the lemon juice and capers. Serve topped with the extra thyme sprigs and sprinkled with black pepper.

MUSSELS WITH WHITE WINE, FENNEL AND TARRAGON

INGREDIENTS

1 large bulb of fennel (with fronds)
coconut oil
2 cloves of garlic, crushed
1 glass (approx. 6 ounces) dry white wine
2 pounds mussels, cleaned and debearded
a handful of fresh tarragon leaves,
   chopped
juice of 1 lemon

Cut the fennel in half lengthwise. Finely chop one half, then, using a mandolin, very finely slice the other half lengthwise into ribbons. Heat 1 tablespoon of coconut oil in a wok or medium-size saucepan with a lid. Add the chopped fennel and garlic and fry for 3 to 4 minutes. Add the wine, let it sizzle for 30 seconds, then throw in the mussels and the ribbons of fennel. Place the lid on the pan and steam for 3 minutes, then give the pan a shake, remove the lid and stir. Discard any mussels that remain closed. Add the tarragon and lemon juice.

FRAGRANT COCONUT-MILK MUSSELS

INGREDIENTS

coconut oil
a thumb-sized piece of ginger,
  roughly sliced
2 cloves of garlic, crushed
3 stalks of lemongrass, bruised
8 spring onions, trimmed and sliced
  at an angle
1 x 13.5-ounce can of coconut milk
1 tablespoon fresh turmeric, grated
1 tablespoon fish sauce
2 pounds mussels, cleaned and debearded
4 stalks of young chard, leaves and
  stalks separated, roughly chopped
juice of 1 lime
a handful of fresh cilantro leaves, chopped

Heat 1 tablespoon coconut oil in a wok or medium-size saucepan with a lid. Add the ginger, garlic, lemongrass and 4 of the spring onions and fry for 5 to 10 minutes to release the aromas. Add the coconut milk, fresh turmeric and fish sauce. Simmer for 10 minutes to infuse the flavors, then strain the liquid through a sieve into a bowl and discard the bits that remain.

Return the liquid to the pan, bring to a simmer again and throw in the mussels and chard. Place the lid on the pan and steam for 3 minutes, then give the pan a shake, remove the lid and stir. Discard any mussels that remain closed. Add the lime juice and the remaining spring onions. Garnish with the cilantro leaves, and serve immediately.

ASIAN-STYLE MUSSELS

INGREDIENTS

coconut oil
5 spring onions, trimmed and sliced at
  an angle
1–2 fresh green or red chilies, deseeded
3 cloves of garlic, crushed
1 glass (approx. 6 ounces) of water or dry
  white wine
2 pounds mussels, cleaned and debearded
1 tablespoon coconut aminos or tamari
1 tablespoon mirin
juice of 1 lime
a handful of fresh Thai basil leaves,
  cilantro or micro herbs, to serve

Heat 1 tablespoon coconut oil in a wok or medium-size saucepan with a lid. Add most of the spring onions, with the chilies and garlic and fry for 3 to 4 minutes. Add the water or wine, let it sizzle for 30 seconds, then throw in the mussels. Season with the coconut aminos and mirin. Place the lid on the pan and steam for 3 minutes, then give the pan a shake, remove the lid and stir. Discard any mussels that remain closed. Add the lime juice and remaining spring onions. Garnish with a few leaves of Thai basil, cilantro or micro herbs, to serve.

Chapter 4
ON THE GO

Chapter 4 /
ON THE GO

_____

Hard-boiled eggs with watercress pesto

Chickpea and eggplant salad

Chickpea salad with cherry tomatoes and avocado

Rice paper wraps with almond dipping sauce:
Crab and pink grapefruit / Chicken and red quinoa /
Salmon and avocado / jumbo shrimp and cucumber

Chicken skewers

Super green soup with cashew cream

Salads in jars: Going green / Anytime jar /
Winter jar / Summer jar

Purple sprouting broccoli with peanut sauce

Boy George's raw soup

Gazpacho

Olive and rosemary chickpea flatbreads

Healthy bites

Grab-and-go chia pot

I always say to my clients that if they leave the house without food, it's a dangerous world out there. We all know that feeling: maybe we left for work in the morning without eating anything, or we worked through lunch and need to eat something quickly before the next meeting. Or perhaps on the weekend we're out and, having had a small breakfast, we suddenly find ourselves hungry and desperate for something quick to quiet our growling stomachs.

Over the years I've talked through these scenarios with my clients and they always tell me that when faced with this kind of situation they buy a muffin, some chips or a sandwich. The processed-snack market is booming worldwide because the food manufacturers know that many of us lead busy lives and just want something quick to eat when we're on the go, whether we're at a train station, an airport, a gas station, newsstand, cafe or coffee shop. They know that most of us leave the house without any real food to sustain us, so they mass-produce the processed kind to keep us going.

This chapter is about outsmarting those food manufacturers. It's about inspiring you to never leave the house without real, nourishing and delicious food to sustain you on whatever journey you're on, so that you don't have to rely on all the junk out there. It's about taking pride in wanting to be healthy and eating proper food, rather than relying on the food manufacturers to feed us (remember they're interested in making money, not in making us healthy).

Taking our own food out with us when we leave should be just as important as packing a bag or preparing a child's packed lunch. Putting in that extra time to prepare our food needs to move up our list of priorities.

Some people may react negatively when you bring out your own homemade meals in a work meeting, on a plane or in a train car, but rather than worrying about what others think, prioritize your health and how you feel. I feel so much better when I don't eat plane food, or buffet food or canapés. The food I take with me when I'm out and about—which I'm going to share with you in this chapter— doesn't taste bland or leave me feeling bloated. So I'm never embarrassed to say to people that I've brought my own food because it shows I care about myself and my health. And nowadays, rather than snickering, most people ask me to email them the recipe because they like the look of what I'm having far more than the limp-looking sandwich on their own plate.

One of the most important things to consider about food on the go is how to transport it. Getting to lunchtime only to find your food in a soggy, warm mess at the bottom of your bag defeats the purpose, so being smart about your containers is crucial. After years of trying all sorts of different options, I've settled on using Mason jars (glass jars you can buy online, in supermarkets or home stores) or any old jar with a secure lid. They're an ideal way to carry any food, and I put leftovers in them most evenings ready for the next day when I'm traveling or out for the day. A lot of people think glass is not very practical as they fear dropping and smashing it, but this has never happened to me. You just need a good bag to carry the jar in, then you can pop it in the fridge when you get to work or wherever you're going. I also have a tiny little ice pack that I use to keep food cool if I'm going to be out all day. I have to throw the ice pack away when I go through airport security, but apart from that it travels well.

WHY YOU SHOULDN'T SNACK ON THE GO (OR ANY OTHER TIME FOR THAT MATTER)

One of the most popular types of food to buy on the go is snack food. Readers of my first book will know that I encourage my clients not to snack, and if you haven't read my first book, here's why . . .

When I first became a nutritional therapist it was common practice to preach snacking. We were told—and we taught our clients—that snacking helps keep blood-sugar levels steady, which reduces sugar cravings, and it keeps you from becoming so hungry between meals that you dive into the cookie jar. Mainstream advice was to eat little and often.

But in 2008 I attended a lecture about blood-sugar management and the lecturer—Leo Pruimboom, from the Natura Foundation—told the room that a healthy body simply doesn't need to snack. We all gasped slightly because it went against everything we'd been taught, but then he explained why and it just made sense—it was a real lightbulb moment for me.

He explained that our current snacking habits—eating something small a couple of hours after breakfast and again after lunch—create permanently elevated levels of the hormone insulin. This drip-feed-of-food way of eating puts our bodies into fat-storage mode all day long.

He went on to say that while sugary snacks (cookies, muffins, chocolate bars, etc.) are the worst culprits, even healthy snacks (like nuts and chopped vegetables or fruit) are unnecessary and still raise insulin levels.

One study, from the Academic Medical Centre in Amsterdam, found that snackers have more abdominal fat (which has been linked to elevated insulin) than non-snackers. Both groups of study participants ate the same amount of food overall in a day, but the non-snackers consumed those calories in three meals with nothing in between.

Another study—published in the health journal *Appetite*—found that people who don't snack eat the same amount at mealtimes as snackers, disproving the myth that if you don't eat between meals you'll binge when you do eat. This is especially true if you eat healthy, balanced meals. So rather than eating a tiny breakfast and then snacking mid morning, just eat a proper breakfast. There really is no need to snack between meals and I never do it myself.

I also believe that our deeply ingrained snacking habits have made us all forget what hunger feels like. I don't encourage anybody to starve themselves, but many of my new clients have never allowed themselves to feel hungry before a meal. They graze all day long, even snacking as they cook dinner, and they've forgotten how it feels to sit down to a meal with a genuine hunger that makes their food taste even more delicious. That's what nature intended—for you to feel hunger and for your food to be all the more satisfying as a result. Mindless, non-stop eating is exhausting your body rather than fueling it.

The only time I do say it is OK to snack is when you are traveling or if you are stuck at work and don't have access to a proper meal. When you first give up snacking you may find yourself very hungry between meals, in which case have a snack if you must, but then look at improving your three main meals. Do this by avoiding sugar (it makes you hungrier), always include protein and fat with your meals, and always have a good breakfast because it sets up your eating for the day.

HARD-BOILED EGGS WITH WATERCRESS PESTO

Hard-boiled eggs are the perfect travel companions. Well, OK, not the smell in the train car but they are a fail-safe healthy option to take with you when out and about. Cook them the night before and leave to cool overnight—couldn't be simpler!

You can now buy hard-boiled eggs and spinach bowls in lots of places in central London, but I prefer to eat mine with a little pot of homemade pesto. Watercress works particularly well with eggs, as does mashed avocado with a squeeze of lemon juice.

INGREDIENTS

2 eggs, preferably free-range or organic

For the watercress pesto:
⅓ pound watercress
juice and zest of ½ a lemon
optional: 1 clove of garlic
⅜ cup pine nuts or cashew nuts
2 teaspoons capers
1 tablespoon extra virgin olive oil
sea salt and freshly ground black pepper

Put the eggs into a pan of cold water and bring to a gentle boil for 7 minutes. Remove from the pan and leave to cool.

Put all the ingredients for the pesto into a blender and blend until smooth. (This will make more pesto than you need for two eggs but it will keep for a few days in the fridge with a thin layer of olive oil on top.)

Dip your shelled hard-boiled eggs into the pesto.

CHICKPEA AND EGGPLANT SALAD

The subtly flavored salads on this page and the next really celebrate the chickpea, which is an excellent source of fiber, protein and iron, and perfect for keeping us going on busy days. Chickpeas really travel well, which is why I've included them in this chapter, but go easy on beans—they are still starchy carbohydrates despite their protein content. So bear this in mind if weight loss is your goal.

INGREDIENTS

½ a small red onion, finely sliced
1 large eggplant, cut in half lengthwise and
    sliced into thin half moons
a good glug of extra virgin olive oil
juice and zest of 1 lemon
2 x 13.5-ounce cans of chickpeas, drained
    and rinsed
2 large fresh tomatoes
1 bunch of fresh parsley, chopped
2 teaspoons garlic-infused olive oil
1 teaspoon cayenne pepper
sea salt and freshly ground black pepper
slivered almonds, to serve

Cover the onion with water and set aside for half an hour—this reduces the harshness of its taste when eaten raw.

Next prepare the eggplant. Spread the half-moon slices out on a baking sheet and brush them with olive oil. Place on a high rack under the broiler for 5 minutes, then take out and brush again with a mixture of olive oil and lemon juice—you can make it quite wet, as the eggplant will absorb all the liquid. Place back under the broiler until the edges of the slices are slightly blackened and the flesh is soft. Set aside in a large bowl.

On the same baking sheet, spread out the chickpeas and broil until they're golden. Add them to the bowl of eggplant.

Dice the tomatoes into small cubes and add to the bowl along with the parsley, drained red onion slices, garlic oil, cayenne pepper, remaining lemon juice, zest, salt and pepper and mix well. Serve warm, with a sprinkling of slivered almonds.

CHICKPEA SALAD WITH CHERRY TOMATOES AND AVOCADO

This has been my staple travel salad for years! Trust me, everyone else around you will be very jealous. Unlike the chickpea recipe on the previous page, this recipe requires absolutely no cooking. It's the ultimate time-is-of-the-essence recipe which can be put together extremely quickly.

INGREDIENTS

1 x 13.5-ounce can of chickpeas, drained
   and rinsed
zest and juice of 1 lemon
a handful of cherry tomatoes,
   cut into halves
½ a red onion, finely diced
1 avocado, peeled, pitted and chopped
a pinch of smoked paprika or dried
   chili flakes
1 tablespoon capers, rinsed
a large handful of lamb's lettuce
   or arugula leaves
a good drizzle of extra virgin olive oil
sea salt and freshly ground black pepper

Mix all the ingredients together and serve. I often make this to take with me when traveling, so I decant it into a jar or a non-plastic container with a lid.

RICE PAPER WRAPS

These little gluten-free wraps are full of delicious and nutritious ingredients and are perfect for taking with you on the go. I've given you four filling options, so take your pick from crab, chicken, salmon or jumbo shrimp—you will find the method on the next page. The chewy texture of the wraps is complemented perfectly by the fresh crunch of the matchsticked vegetables, giving you mouthfuls of goodness in each bite. Lovely when dipped into the creamy almond sauce on page 137 with a hit of lime for extra zing, but as always, mix it up and make up your own versions.

INGREDIENTS

CRAB AND PINK GRAPEFRUIT:
½ pound white crab meat or crayfish tails
1 pink grapefruit, peeled, cut into segments and very gently dried between paper towels
½ a cucumber, cut into matchsticks
10 stalks of extra-fine asparagus, blanched
a handful of fresh Thai basil, mint and cilantro leaves, chopped

CHICKEN AND RED QUINOA:
1 chicken breast, poached, shredded and seasoned
1 spring onion, cut into matchsticks
1 red pepper, cut into matchsticks
zest of ½ a lemon (toss the chicken in the zest before making the rolls, so that it is evenly distributed)
skin of 1 preserved lemon, cut into matchsticks
½ cup cooked red quinoa
a handful of fresh basil, dill, cilantro, mint and parsley leaves, chopped
a handful of crunchy lettuce leaves, sliced

SALMON AND AVOCADO:
2 salmon fillets, seasoned with salt, poached, skinned and flaked
½ an avocado, finely sliced
¼ a red cabbage, finely sliced
½ a yellow pepper, cut into matchsticks
½ a red pepper, cut into matchsticks
½ a carrot, cut into matchsticks
½ an apple, cut into matchsticks
1 spring onion, cut into strips
a handful of fresh basil, parsley, cilantro leaves and chives, chopped

JUMBO SHRIMP AND CUCUMBER:
½ pound cooked jumbo shrimp (about 3 shrimp per roll)
1 carrot, cut into matchsticks
a thumb-sized piece of fresh ginger, peeled and cut into matchsticks
½ a cucumber, cut into matchsticks
1 yellow pepper, cut into matchsticks
a handful of fresh cilantro and mint leaves, chopped
a handful of crunchy lettuce leaves, sliced

Optional extras:
crushed cashews
alfalfa sprouts
China Rose radish sprouts
bean sprouts

How to roll your wraps:

Prepare your ingredients and lay them out on a dish. Prepare a plastic chopping board if you have one—plastic works better than wood, as the rice paper is quite sticky—or work on a clean tea towel and fill a large, shallow dish with warm water.

Take a wrap and soak it for 5 seconds in the water, then lay it out on the chopping board or work surface—it will still feel quite hard but will soften as you go. Place your ingredients horizontally at the bottom or center of the wrap, packing them as tightly together as possible. Take the right and left edges of the wrap, and fold them in. Take the bottom of the wrap and roll it upward, taking the ingredients with it. Try to wrap them as tightly as possible, then leave the wrap sealed side down.

Place on a plate, and repeat. Try not to let the wraps touch each other as you make them or they will stick together as they dry.

Serve with the almond dipping sauce.

ALMOND DIPPING SAUCE

INGREDIENTS

3 tablespoons crunchy almond butter
2 teaspoons coconut aminos or tamari
juice of 2 limes
1 teaspoon maple syrup or coconut syrup
a few thin strips of spring onion
red chili slices, crushed roasted peanuts
  and mint leaves, to garnish

To make the sauce, mix together all the ingredients until they come together smoothly, then add 1 tablespoon of water at a time until the sauce reaches a dipping consistency and sprinkle the garnishes over top.

CHICKEN SKEWERS

Skewers are the perfect on-the-go food option as they are so portable. Whether out on a weekend picnic, or making your lunch for the office, it doesn't take long to put these together. They should ideally be eaten hot but are equally good if served cold. The subtle tartness of the lemon slices, combined with the sweetness of the fennel, goes so well with chicken.

INGREDIENTS

1 chicken breast, cut into 8–12 pieces
zest and juice of 1 lemon
2 teaspoons coconut aminos
1 tablespoon olive oil
1 lemon, cut into thin slices
1 teaspoon crystallized coconut
1 small yellow or green zucchini (½ cup), cut into ½-inch slices
1 small red onion, cut into small wedges
1 small bulb of fennel, cut into small wedges
1 tablespoon chopped fresh flat-leaf parsley, to serve

Put the chicken pieces in a bowl with the lemon zest and juice, coconut aminos and olive oil. Cover and set aside for at least half an hour, longer if possible. (The chicken can also be marinated the day before and put in the fridge overnight.)

Bring a small pan of water to a boil, and simmer the lemon slices for 2 to 3 minutes to remove some of the bitterness. Drain, then sprinkle the slices with the crystallized coconut.

Thread the chicken pieces onto 4 long skewers, alternating with the lemon and zucchini slices and the red onion and fennel wedges. (If you are using wooden skewers, soak them in cold water for 30 minutes before assembling to make sure they don't burn during cooking.)

Heat a griddle pan or the broiler to medium-high heat. Cook the skewers for 15 minutes, turning occasionally, until the chicken is cooked through and the vegetables are softened and charred. Serve immediately, sprinkled with the parsley.

SUPER GREEN SOUP WITH CASHEW CREAM

This simple soup really is a celebration of all things green. Zucchini, kale and leeks also work well, along with any other greens from the fridge that need using up. The cashew cream plays a lovely trick on your taste buds.

INGREDIENTS

olive oil
1 onion, chopped
1 head of broccoli, cut into florets
3 handfuls of fresh or frozen peas
3½ cups vegetable or chicken stock
1 x 12-ounce small bag of baby spinach
optional: a small handful of fresh
   parsley, chopped
optional: 1 green chili, chopped

For the cashew cream:
5 ounces raw cashews
1¼ cups hot water
1 clove of garlic
zest of 1 lemon

A few hours before making this soup, prepare the cashew cream. Put the cashews into a bowl, pour the hot water over and leave to soak for at least 2 hours. Once the cashews are tender, drain and put into a food processor, along with 1¼ cups fresh water, the garlic and lemon zest, and mix until completely smooth and creamy. Set aside.

Heat 1 tablespoon olive oil in a large saucepan, and sweat the onion until translucent. Add the broccoli and peas to the pan, cook for 5 minutes, then add the stock—the vegetables should be just covered (you may need to add a little extra water). Bring to a boil, then simmer until the broccoli is tender, roughly 4 minutes. Don't overcook the vegetables or they will turn a dull green.

Using an immersion blender, start blending the soup, adding a handful of spinach at a time—the spinach will cook as it's mixed into the soup. Blend until the soup is smooth and thick, then stir through half the cashew cream.

Serve in bowls with a swirl of cashew cream on top and fresh parsley and chili, if using, sprinkled over.

"WHEN DIET IS WRONG,
MEDICINE IS OF NO USE.
WHEN DIET IS RIGHT,
MEDICINE IS OF NO NEED."

AYURVEDIC PROVERB

SALADS IN JARS

For me, these salads are the perfect on-the-go meal. Vibrant, delicious and so easy to prepare, they're a great alternative to any lackluster coffee-shop sandwich. Guaranteed freshness all year round, salad jars aren't just for sunny picnics in the park. Seek out seasonal ingredients and be creative—just make sure to layer sensibly, with leafy greens on top and dressings at the bottom, to avoid any sogginess. To make the dressings, simply combine the ingredients given for each one, and add it to the jar to taste. You might like to reserve half to flavor a later jar if you prefer a milder salad.

SERVES 1

GOING GREEN

INGREDIENTS

Bottom layer (dressing): 1 avocado, chopped or blended / juice of 1 lemon / ½ a clove of garlic, chopped / 1 tablespoon extra virgin olive oil / sea salt

2nd layer: ½–1 Granny Smith apple, diced

3rd layer: 3 tablespoons chopped walnuts

4th layer: a handful of spinach

5th layer: a small handful of steamed broccoli florets

6th layer: a few cucumber ribbons

Top layer: a little fresh mint and parsley, chopped / a grating of lemon zest

SERVES 1

ANYTIME JAR

INGREDIENTS

Bottom layer (dressing): 1 tablespoon extra virgin olive oil / juice of ½ a lemon / a dash of Tabasco / sea salt and freshly ground black pepper

2nd layer: a handful of red and yellow cherry tomatoes, halved

3rd layer: 1 avocado, diced

4th layer: 1 hard-boiled egg, chopped

5th layer: a small handful of watercress

6th layer: a small handful of baby spinach

Top layer: a little fresh parsley, chopped / a few China Rose radish sprouts / a few alfalfa sprouts

WINTER JAR

INGREDIENTS

Bottom layer: 3 tablespoons hummus / sea salt and freshly ground black pepper

2nd layer: a large handful of roasted sweet potato and pumpkin, diced

3rd layer: 5 tablespoons cauliflower rice (see page 302)

4th layer: 2 tablespoons sautéd onion

5th layer: 2 tablespoons pomegranate seeds

Top layer: a handful of kale or spinach, shredded and blanched

SUMMER JAR

INGREDIENTS

Bottom layer (dressing): juice and zest of ½ a lemon / 1 tablespoon white balsamic vinegar / ½ teaspoon mustard powder / 2 tablespoons extra virgin olive oil / a tiny dash of coconut syrup / sea salt and freshly ground black pepper

2nd layer: 2 handfuls of peas, fava beans and sugar snap peas

3rd layer: 1 poached chicken breast, shredded

4th layer: a large handful of finely sliced radishes

Top layer: 1 spring onion, finely chopped / ½–1 green chili, sliced / a little fresh dill, parsley, mint and basil, chopped

PURPLE SPROUTING BROCCOLI WITH PEANUT SAUCE

Purple sprouting broccoli has a wonderful flavor and a long harvesting season, at its best between February and April. I like mine *al dente* and, in this recipe, the peanuts give added crunch. Delicious on their own or as an accompaniment to meat or fish, these tender stems and their luscious leaves are wonderfully versatile.

INGREDIENTS

½ pound purple sprouting broccoli, trimmed
olive oil

For the peanut sauce:
1 cup whole unsalted peanuts, with or without skin
2 mild red chilies, deseeded
2 tablespoons tamari
juice of 1 lime
2 tablespoons garlic-infused olive oil

Blanch the broccoli for 2 minutes, then rinse and leave to dry completely.

To prepare the peanut sauce, pulse the peanuts, chilies, tamari, lime juice and garlic-infused olive oil in a food processor to make a chunky sauce. You might need to loosen it with a tablespoon or two of water.

Drizzle 2 tablespoons of olive oil over the broccoli and mix well to cover. Put a griddle pan over a high heat. Once the pan is hot, grill the broccoli in batches, until charred all over.

Serve the broccoli drizzled with the peanut sauce.

BOY GEORGE'S RAW SOUP

I've been working with Boy George for a few years now and he is a complete joy to talk food with. George naturally leans toward a raw and vegan diet and because he has been so dedicated (and patient!) to learning about his health and what his body needs, he has really managed to get the balance right. He is now well known as the "food police" to his family, friends and colleagues, as he wants to spread his passion for health far and wide, so he is always in his kitchen creating meals to feed his mum or brothers. I take my hat off to him for his commitment to his health—he now even takes a portable steamer on tour! This is a soup he created for his brother and it has now become a staple in all of our lives.

INGREDIENTS

1 cup vegetable stock
1 stick of celery, chopped (reserve a small
    amount to garnish)
½ a small avocado
a thumbnail-sized piece of fresh ginger
¼ teaspoon sea salt
a few peppercorns
½ a Granny Smith apple (reserve a small
    amount to garnish)
½ teaspoon apple cider vinegar
2 tablespoons toasted pumpkin seeds
a drizzle of extra virgin olive oil, to serve

Blend all the ingredients, except the pumpkin seeds, together in a food processor, then cover and chill for half an hour in the fridge. Serve garnished with finely chopped celery and apple, a scattering of toasted pumpkin seeds and a little drizzle of olive oil.

"I LOVE FOOD AND I LOVE COOKING.
AMELIA HAS TAUGHT ME THE FOUNDATIONS
OF HEALTHY EATING SO I CAN STILL ENJOY
MY FOOD WHILST KEEPING HEALTHY."

BOY GEORGE

SERVES 4

GAZPACHO

What's great about this soup is that you get a massive veg-hit without any cooking, basically like a smoothie. This version is gluten-free and I think it lacks nothing for being served without bread.

INGREDIENTS

1 red pepper, deseeded
½ a stick of celery
¼ of a cucumber, deseeded
1 pound firm ripe tomatoes
1 spring onion
½ a clove of garlic
1 handful of fresh basil
1½ teaspoons sherry vinegar
a generous dash of Tabasco
sea salt and freshly ground black pepper
pumpkin seeds and fresh baby basil
  leaves, to garnish

Reserve a very small amount of red pepper, celery and cucumber for the garnish, then mix the rest of the ingredients (apart from the basil and pumpkin seeds) in a food processor until completely smooth (you can leave it a little chunky if you prefer). Season with salt and pepper, and add more sherry vinegar or Tabasco to taste. Leave to chill in the fridge for at least 2 hours.

Chop the reserved red pepper, cucumber and celery into the smallest dice you can. Serve the gazpacho in bowls, topped with the chopped vegetables, pumpkin seeds and baby basil leaves.

OLIVE AND ROSEMARY CHICKPEA FLATBREADS

Chickpea flour is a great gluten-free alternative when it comes to these delicious flatbreads. Make up a batch if traveling, as they are so portable and don't take up much room. I love to eat mine with a little lemon zest and juice, and a drizzle of extra virgin olive oil. They can be spread with or dipped into hummus, pesto or tapenade (see pages 73–5). The rosemary and olives remind me of sunny summer days—the perfect flavor combination.

INGREDIENTS

1⅛ cups chickpea flour
1 cup water
2 tablespoons garlic-infused olive oil
1 sprig of fresh rosemary, leaves picked
sea salt and freshly ground black pepper
⅛ cup pitted green olives, finely sliced
olive oil

Pour the chickpea flour into a bowl and gradually add the water, whisking all the time, until you have a smooth batter. (Alternatively, pulse the flour and water together in a blender or food processor.) Cover and let the batter sit at room temperature for an hour or two, if you have time.

Preheat the oven to 375°F and grease an 8-inch ovenproof frying pan or pizza pan with a little olive oil. (If you don't have an ovenproof frying pan, use an 8-inch solid-bottomed round cake tin.)

When you are ready to cook, stir the garlic-infused olive oil and rosemary leaves into the batter and season well. Pour the batter into the greased pan. Sprinkle the olives on top and bake for 20 to 25 minutes, until the flatbread has set and the sides have started to crisp. Carefully remove from the pan and leave to cool, before cutting into triangles.

HEALTHY BITES

These little bites of goodness are a very useful staple for busy days, particularly when traveling. There are hundreds of recipes out there for similar things, but these two flavor combinations are ones I created a while ago. Remember, they are still high in sugar so portion control must be exercised. You can also leave out the coconut nectar and the honey for a less-sweet flavor. I have made these ingredients optional. I recommend making a large batch and then freezing them.

INGREDIENTS

For cacao bites:
3½ ounces cashew nuts
2½ ounces Medjool dates
1 tablespoon chia seeds
optional: 1 teaspoon coconut nectar
2 tablespoons raw or roasted
   hazelnut butter
1 teaspoon vanilla extract
1 tablespoon raw cacao nibs
¼ teaspoon sea salt
¼ cup raw cacao powder

For orange-and-sesame bites:
3½ ounces cashew nuts
2½ ounces Medjool dates
1 tablespoon chia seeds
optional: 1 teaspoon raw honey
1 teaspoon vanilla extract
2 tablespoons tahini
¼ teaspoon sea salt
3 tablespoons toasted white
   sesame seeds
zest of 2 oranges

Soak the cashew nuts and dates separately in warm filtered water for at least 30 minutes.

Drain the cashews and pulse in a food processor, then add the drained dates and the rest of the ingredients, except the cacao powder or the sesame seeds and orange zest. Blend until you get a smooth-ish paste. Chill the mixture for 45 minutes.

Take a heaped teaspoon of the mixture and roll into a ball—repeat until all the mixture is used. You may need to wash your hands if they get too sticky. Roll the balls in cacao powder (for the cacao bites), dusting off any excess, or sesame seeds and orange zest (for the orange-and-sesame bites) and chill for a few hours before serving.

GRAB-AND-GO CHIA POT

A simple and versatile little recipe—perfect for whipping together the night before and grabbing on your way out in the morning. Get creative with fruit, nuts and seeds to make your perfect pot—a wonderful alternative to any store-bought sugary cereal. The recipe below is the basic method but you can use different fruit instead of the berries and go to town with all sorts of different flavors. Try mango purée, matcha powder, raw cacao powder, mint, lime and pineapple, orange zest and blueberry or fresh figs and hazelnuts. You could also add coconut yogurt.

INGREDIENTS

¼ teaspoon coconut crystals
¼ teaspoon vanilla powder
¼ teaspoon ground cinnamon
1 cup coconut milk (or milk of your choice)
2 tablespoons chia seeds
¼ cup fresh or frozen mixed berries
  (strawberries and cherries work well)
2 teaspoons mixed seeds

Put the coconut crystals, vanilla powder and cinnamon into a 12-ounce jar. Add 2 tablespoons of the milk and mix well. Stir in the rest of the milk and the chia seeds. Top with the mixed berries and seeds and leave to set in the fridge for a few hours or overnight.

Chapter 5

THE NAUGHTY CHAPTER

Chapter 5 /
THE NAUGHTY CHAPTER

———————————

Five-seed gluten-free bread

Pumpkin drop scones

Vanilla-honey ice cream and vanilla milkshake

Lemon, coconut and chia seed cookies

Mini carrot cakes

Chocolate cupcakes with whipped almond butter
and chia seed jam

Peanut butter and jam smoothie

Now I don't have much of a sweet tooth. I don't need cake or muffins in my life, but I haven't always been like this. At one point I was drinking up to ten cups of sugary tea just to get through the day. Having spent a good few years weaning myself off sugar, training my taste buds to be satisfied rather than stimulated and learning to eat smaller quantities, I don't ever want to go back to over-eating. And while it is fantastic that we can make so many naughty things with healthy ingredients and in healthier ways, they still are "naughty" in that we simply don't need so much food or to supplement our three meals a day. Sugar is still sugar, no matter what form it comes in, even something pure like honey or dates. Even the low-glycemic sugars, such as stevia or xylitol, have been found to produce the same effect on our brains as when we eat sugar. Like so many other dietary habits that aren't great for us, eating sweet "treats" has simply become something many of us do without thinking.

That said, working with lots of clients has taught me how different we all are, and I appreciate that many people want to enjoy an occasional dessert. And I'm forever being asked for recipes for sweet treats, which is why I've included this chapter. Please do remember that just because the recipes are in this book does not mean that you can eat them in abundance. They are healthier alternatives to use for special occasions.

I think mindfulness is the key to maneuvering through this chapter. We don't need a dessert every day "just because." It's so important to address our habits, instead of just letting them dictate our everyday behavior. Naturally there are occasions when something sweet might be appropriate, but we don't have to offer dessert every single time we have friends over—sometimes people might be relieved to not have to resist the temptation.

If you're eating a nourishing, filling meal, ask yourself how much extra food you really need. I call this having an internal dialogue. So stop, and have that conversation with yourself. After a big meal, ask yourself: "Do I really need something else to eat?" "Am I eating it out of necessity, out of hunger? Or 'just because'?" "Will it make me feel happy and nourished, or a little bit sick and uncomfortably full?" Ask yourself those questions rather than mindlessly heading for the fridge to get something sugary straight after your dinner. Instead, wait a little while, let your meal digest, drink some water and do something you really enjoy—and see how you feel in twenty minutes.

And if you really must have something, don't go for sugary, processed, ready-made desserts. Try one of these simple, nourishing treats instead . . .

FIVE-SEED GLUTEN-FREE BREAD

I don't usually tend to supplement soups or salads with bread, but it's nice to know that there's a delicious, gluten-free option available for those odd occasions. I've tried many bread recipes and this is the one that works for me—loaded with seeds, it delivers a brilliant rise and a great crust. Although it only lasts for a day at its best, it's also delicious toasted for a couple more after that.

INGREDIENTS

1⅓ cups almond milk, plus extra
  for brushing
2 large eggs, preferably free-range
  or organic
1 teaspoon cider apple vinegar
1½ cups gluten-free brown bread flour,
  plus extra for dusting
1½ cups teff flour
½ teaspoon fine pink Himalayan salt
2 tablespoons coconut blossom nectar
1 tablespoon fast-acting yeast
1 tablespoon each of pumpkin, sesame,
  sunflower and flaxseeds (plus extra for
  decorating the top of the loaf)
1 tablespoon chia seeds
3 tablespoons melted coconut oil

Preheat the oven to 400°F and lightly oil a baking sheet.

Pour the almond milk into a small pan and place over low heat for a couple of minutes or until warm to the touch. Remove from the heat and leave to cool slightly. Crack the eggs into a large bowl, add the vinegar, then gradually stir in the warm milk.

Combine the flours, salt, coconut blossom nectar, yeast and seeds (but do reserve some for the top) in another bowl, then, using a wooden spoon, stir the dry ingredients into the wet mixture until a sticky dough is formed. Add the melted coconut oil, then bring it together with your hands into a ball, dusting with a little flour to prevent it from being too sticky.

Place on the baking sheet, score a cross on top with a sharp knife, brush with a little almond milk and scatter liberally with the reserved seeds. Cover with a damp tea towel, then leave to rise in a warm place for around 1 hour, or until doubled in size.

Once the dough has risen, brush with a little almond milk or beaten egg and scatter the remaining seeds on top. Put the tray into the hot oven and bake for 35 minutes, or until the bread is golden and cooked through. Tap the base with your hand: if it sounds hollow, it is done. Leave to cool slightly on a wire rack, then slice and serve.

PUMPKIN DROP SCONES

Drop scones but with a seasonal twist. I love pumpkin and the subtle sweetness it adds to this recipe. You really don't need many of these to fill you up and coconut yogurt is the perfect accompaniment.

INGREDIENTS

1 cup cooked pumpkin (or about 8 ounces raw pumpkin flesh, steamed until tender)
2/3 cup gluten-free oats
2 medium eggs, preferably free-range or organic
½ heaped teaspoon baking powder
1 tablespoon maple syrup
½ teaspoon ground cinnamon
a generous pinch of sea salt
coconut oil

To serve:
4 tablespoons coconut yogurt
3 tablespoons slivered almonds, toasted
2–4 tablespoons maple syrup

Put the pumpkin, oats, eggs, baking powder, maple syrup, cinnamon and salt into a blender and pulse to a smooth batter.

Heat 1 teaspoon coconut oil in a non-stick frying pan over medium heat. When the oil is hot, add a large spoonful of the batter to the pan, making a pancake of about 2 inches in diameter.

Depending on the size of your pan, you should manage to cook about 4 scones in each batch. Cook for 2 to 3 minutes, or until bubbles have formed on the surface and the top is almost set, then flip the scones over and cook them on the other side for a further 2 to 3 minutes. Cool on a wire rack while you cook the rest of the batter the same way.

Serve topped with a dollop of coconut yogurt, a sprinkle of slivered almonds and some maple syrup drizzled over the top.

STAGE ONE / *Ingredients*

STAGE TWO / *Freeze*

STAGE THREE / *Assemble*

STAGE FOUR / *Eat*

VANILLA-HONEY ICE CREAM AND VANILLA MILKSHAKE

Traditional, good-quality ice cream is not such a bad product—it tends to be the cheaper varieties that have lots of sugar and processed rubbish added to them. Here is the healthiest, dairy-free version of ice cream that I could make. I recommend serving a small dollop with fresh fruit as an occasional treat or at a dinner party—a little every so often.

For a really smooth, creamy texture, this is best made with a Vitamix, but you can also use a heavy-duty food processor, which will give a more granular finish.

INGREDIENTS

For the ice cream:
2 cups almond milk
10 ounces soaked cashews
2/3 cup raw honey
seeds from 2 vanilla pods
1 tablespoon vanilla extract
1 tablespoon lecithin
½ teaspoon sea salt

For one milkshake:
1 cup vanilla ice cream
1 cup almond milk
½ cup strawberries

Blend all the ice cream ingredients in a Vitamix or heavy-duty food processor until smooth. Or place all the ingredients into a table blender or a large jug and blend until smooth using an immersion blender. Then place the blended mixture in an ice-cream maker and follow the instructions.

If you don't have an ice-cream machine, pour the mixture into a container and place in the freezer. Remove after 2 hours and stir thoroughly with a fork before returning to the freezer until frozen.

Once you have the ice cream perfected, you can go ahead and try a milkshake. Simply blend all the ingredients together.

LEMON, COCONUT AND CHIA SEED COOKIES

I know many people who can't drink a cup of tea without a cookie. Naturally, I don't endorse the need for treats or regularly eating sweet things. But if you are going to have the occasional cookie, a lovingly prepared homemade one is the best choice. The addition of almond flour and chia seeds provides a source of protein and omega-3 healthy fat, which makes these cookies less dangerous than those from a package.

INGREDIENTS

1 cup almond flour, plus extra
  for dusting
⅓ cup coconut flour
½ teaspoon baking powder
2 tablespoons chia seeds
a pinch of sea salt
7 tablespoons coconut butter
½ cup coconut palm sugar
zest and juice of 1 lemon
1 teaspoon vanilla extract
2 eggs, preferably free-range or
  organic, beaten
coconut oil, for greasing

Preheat the oven to 325°F. Lightly grease one or two baking sheets with coconut oil.

Mix the almond flour, coconut flour, baking powder, chia seeds and sea salt together in a bowl.

In a blender, mix the coconut butter and coconut palm sugar together until well combined and not crumbly. Add the lemon zest and juice and the vanilla extract and mix together. Gradually mix in the beaten eggs. Fold the wet mixture into the dry flour mixture until combined, being careful not to overwork.

On a lightly floured surface, roll the biscuit dough out to approximately ¼ inch thick. Using a 2½-inch cutter, stamp out 30 circles. The dough can be rerolled to use it all up.

Put the circles on to the baking sheets and bake in the oven for 10 to 12 minutes, until golden brown and crisp around the edges. Remove from the oven and allow to rest for a few minutes before transferring to a wire rack to cool.

MINI CARROT CAKES

If I were going to eat cake, it would always be carrot cake. This is a slightly healthier twist on an old-fashioned version, made in miniature sizes so you don't overindulge.

INGREDIENTS

For the cakes:
2 cups almond flour
½ teaspoon baking soda
3 teaspoons ground cinnamon
3 teaspoons ground ginger
a pinch of sea salt
a pinch of vanilla powder or
  ½ teaspoon of vanilla extract
6 medium carrots, washed
  (unpeeled) and finely grated
2 medium eggs, preferably
  free-range or organic, whisked
1 x 10-ounce can of coconut milk
1 teaspoon coconut syrup

For the icing:
1 cup no-aroma coconut butter
  (not oil)—remove from the fridge
  10 minutes before using
juice of 1 orange, zest of 2 oranges,
  with some kept aside to garnish
a pinch of vanilla powder or a teaspoon
  of vanilla extract

Preheat the oven to 400°F. Line a tray with 20 cupcake liners.

Mix the dry ingredients together in one bowl. Mix the carrots, eggs and coconut milk together in another. Combine the wet and dry mixtures and spoon into the liners—you can fill them to the top, as these cakes don't rise very much.

Cook for 30 minutes, until they are golden and a skewer comes out clean when inserted into the middle. Then leave to cool on a wire rack.

To make the icing, whisk all the ingredients together until smooth, reserving a little of the zest to sprinkle over the top. Spread the icing on top of each cooled cake with a knife. Put the cakes into the fridge for 10 minutes for the icing to firm up, then serve decorated with the reserved zest.

CHOCOLATE CUPCAKES WITH WHIPPED ALMOND BUTTER AND CHIA SEED JAM

Everybody seems to love a cupcake so I thought I should include a recipe, but these are less sweet, very much lighter and oh so much more nutritious—a clean version of a dirty old classic.

INGREDIENTS

For the chia seed jam:
1 cup raspberries or strawberries
2½ tablespoons chia seeds

For the cupcakes:
½ cup coconut flour
1 teaspoon baking soda
a pinch of vanilla powder or 1 teaspoon of vanilla extract
2 tablespoons organic dark cocoa powder
2 tablespoons melted coconut oil
2 eggs, preferably free-range or organic
3 tablespoons agave syrup or coconut blossom nectar
⅓ cup coconut milk

For the whipped almond butter:
⅓ cup almond butter
2 tablespoons maple syrup
1½ tablespoons coconut cream

First, make the chia seed jam. Pulse the berries and chia seeds in a blender, and put into a bowl to rest in the fridge for a minimum of 2 hours.

Preheat the oven to 400°F. Line a cupcake tray with 6 paper liners.

Mix together the dry cake ingredients. Add the coconut oil, eggs and syrup, and mix well with a wooden spoon. Slowly add the coconut milk, stirring continuously, until you get a smooth, fairly runny batter.

Pour the batter into the paper liners and bake in the oven for 18 to 20 minutes, or until a wooden skewer comes out clean when inserted into the middle of a cupcake. Remove the cakes from the tray and leave to cool on a wire rack.

While the cakes cool, make the topping. Put the almond butter into a large bowl, and begin to whip with a fork. Add the maple syrup and mix well. Then use a handheld mixer to whip the butter as you slowly add the coconut cream. The mixture should become light and fluffy. Refrigerate for 30 minutes.

To assemble, cut a small, shallow hole out of the top of each cupcake and fill with the chia seed jam. Top with the whipped almond butter and serve immediately.

PEANUT BUTTER AND JAM SMOOTHIE

This is something I created for Sam Smith, who loves the classic American combination of peanut butter and jam. This slightly healthier form of these flavors is just as yummy.

INGREDIENTS

1½ cups fresh or frozen strawberries
   or raspberries
2 tablespoons smooth, sugar-free
   peanut butter
½ an avocado, peeled, pitted and
   roughly chopped
1 teaspoon coconut syrup
1 cup almond milk
a handful of ice cubes

Put all the ingredients in a blender. Pulse at first to break up the ice cubes, then blend until you have a smooth drink.

Chapter 6

FRIENDLY FATS

Chapter 6 /
FRIENDLY FATS

Crunchy nut and seed granola

Grilled sardines and tomatoes with
a crunchy herb dressing

Avocado soufflé

Spiced seeds

Tuna tartare with crunchy avocado

Salmon balls with crunchy white sauce

Duck with beans and greens

Simple sardine salad

Winter oxtail stew with pumpkin and kale

Parsnip and ginger mash

Spiced coconut crème anglaise with
pineapple and goji berries

Get your greens:
Green smoothie / Green milk

Since the seventies we've been hearing the very clear message that fats will make us fat and give us heart disease. "The Seven Countries Study," first published in 1970, looked into fat intake and incidences of heart disease and seemed to prove a link. But it's since been found that the study was flawed. First, it didn't take into account other factors (like smoking), and it also left out data that contradicted the author's belief that fat was unhealthy. For example, certain countries like France, Switzerland and Sweden, where diets were high in fat and yet the rates of heart disease were low, were omitted. Anyway, we were advised to swap pure fats like those in butter and red meat for margarine and low-fat processed foods. But what these foods lacked in fat they made up for in preservatives, additives and sugar.

The message (however misguided) went out and governments soon made fat a matter of public health policy. Guidelines and food pyramids were drawn up that recommended we greatly reduce our intake of high-fat foods like butter, red meat and eggs to reduce the risk of heart disease.

But, as is often the way with health advice, the message got a little confused. Rather than cutting down on high-fat foods and opting for naturally low-fat ones like protein, fruits and vegetables, people went for factory-made low-fat foods. We began eating more yogurts, bread, low-fat spreads, ready-made meals, pasta and cereal than ever before—and we began getting fatter. Why? Because all those foods are forms of sugar and sugar is the devil in disguise in this fat-phobic scenario.

The good news is the tide has started to change. Study after study has shown that sugar is bad for us, and that over-consumption can increase our risk of heart disease, diabetes and premature aging, and sabotage our energy levels. The anti-sugar message is out there and that's a great thing, because we're starting to reduce our sugar intake in the same way we started to reduce our fat intake over thirty years ago.

And as reducing sugar intake has taken center stage, the good news is that fat has been firmly put back on the menu. We no longer need to fear fat: there is more and more research to support the fact that fats won't make us fat or give us heart disease in the way we were once told they would.

To be clear, studies have shown that natural fat—in moderation—is a really important part of a healthy diet. Eggs—previously thought to raise our cholesterol levels and increase our risk of heart disease—have been found to do no such thing. They're full of the healthy kind of cholesterol and are a fantastic source of protein, selenium, vitamin D, zinc and iron.

Other naturally high-fat foods like oily fish, nuts, seeds, oils and avocados have been found to be equally nourishing, containing all sorts of heart- and health-protecting goodness. And even saturated fat has been let off the health hook. In 2014, scientists from Cambridge University in the U.K. and Harvard University in the U.S. conducted a meta-analysis (a study of other studies) and found no link between saturated fat and heart disease—and raised many concerns over the accuracy of the infamous Seven Countries Study.

So the message that fat is OK—and that sugar is not—is out and now it's just taking time for this to filter into the mainstream. Our bodies need fat to maintain our cell structure, and fat has been shown to protect brain health, joints and immunity and to boost energy levels. It keeps us feeling full (whereas incredibly low- or no-fat diets leave us hungry and low in energy). Fat also helps our bodies to absorb other nutrients more efficiently, like the antioxidant lycopene, found in brightly colored foods like tomatoes.

So don't fear fat. Having said that, I often find that messages about food are followed without thought and taken to extremes. Back in the seventies when we were told not to eat fat, we simply swapped fats for carbohydrates like bread and pasta to the extent that we now eat them by the bucketload.

What I'm trying to say is that when it comes to health messages, moderation is the key. Knowing that fats are actually healthy doesn't give you the go-ahead to eat handful after handful of Brazil nuts, or have bacon for breakfast every morning, load your salads up with several sources of fat or eat endless amounts of cheese.

Be smart about your fats. Buy the best you can afford and savor it once or twice a week, instead of eating cheaper sources daily. When it comes to animal products, organic is always preferable. Enjoy a good mix of fats because different types have different health benefits (see page 187). And, as always, variety is key, so choose different fat sources for each meal.

Fat really does enhance the flavor and hence our enjoyment of food, but remember that fat, like everything else, should be eaten mindfully and with grace.

YOUR GUIDE TO NOURISHING FATS

UNSATURATED FATS

These have been shown to help improve heart health. There are two types:

- Monounsaturated: found in olives, nuts, avocados and seeds.
- Polyunsaturated: found in sunflower and flaxseed oils, walnuts and fish.

FATTY ACIDS

These are a type of polyunsaturated fat:

- Omega-3: most people have heard of this one, an essential fatty acid that plays a role in brain function and heart health. Good sources include fatty fish, like salmon, mackerel, sardines and tuna, plus Brazil nuts, walnuts, pumpkin and chia seeds and green vegetables.
- Omega-6: a lesser-known fatty acid, but with just as many health benefits as omega-3. Good sources include nuts, seeds, green leafy vegetables and oils like olive, hempseed and sesame.
- Omega-9: this is a non-essential fatty acid because the body produces it naturally, but only when it's getting enough omega-3 and omega-6. Omega-9 protects heart health and immunity and is found in avocados, almonds, hazelnuts, pistachios, cashews and olive oil.

SATURATED FATS

These are found mostly in animal products, such as meat, cheese and butter. Certain meats, like chicken and fish, contain less saturated fat than others, like lamb or beef. Saturated fat is also found in coconut oil. And of course it's also found in processed foods like cakes, ice cream, cookies and take-out pizza. The key is to get your saturated fats from natural, real foods—because of its rich flavor and taste you'll only need a little in your meal. Avoid it in the form of processed foods, like cakes and cookies.

CRUNCHY NUT AND SEED GRANOLA

I'm really not a fan of cereal, but for those of you that like to start your day with a little bit of crunch, this is for you. Full of healthy fats and rich in nutrients, this will help to keep you full as well as providing an energy boost. Suitable for any time of the day.

INGREDIENTS

1 cup dates
½ cup figs
¼ cup dried mulberries, raisins
  or prunes
2/3 cup chia seeds
1 1/3 cups almonds
2/3 cup cashews
2/3 cup macadamia nuts
optional: 2/3 cup desiccated coconut
1 tablespoon vanilla extract
1 tablespoon sea salt

Soak the dried fruit overnight in ¾ cup water. Then blend with their soaking water, and add the chia seeds.

Soak the nuts in salted water overnight, then discard the water and pulse the nuts in a food processor.

Combine the chopped nuts and dried-fruit mixture with your hands, and add the desiccated coconut, vanilla extract and salt.

Spread the mixture out on one or two baking sheets and bake overnight, or until it is dry, at 175°F with the oven door slightly open.

When cool, break the granola up into chunks and store in an airtight container. Serve with nut milk or coconut yogurt and fresh berries.

A few alternative flavors to try adding into the mix:
◆ Banana and passion fruit
◆ Fig and raspberry
◆ Pear and grape

GRILLED SARDINES AND TOMATOES WITH A CRUNCHY HERB DRESSING

Sardines are a rich source of the omega-3 essential fatty acids EPA and DPA, and they contain a wealth of nutrients, including vitamin D, which is essential for optimal health. So serve this dish any time of day and enjoy this king of the sea.

INGREDIENTS

For the dressing:
3 shallots (approx. ¼ cup), finely chopped
2 tablespoons red wine vinegar
a small bunch of fresh marjoram
a small bunch of fresh parsley
1 cup yellow, red and green peppers, deseeded
½ cup cucumber, peeled and deseeded
2 tablespoons extra virgin olive oil
1 tablespoon fish sauce
juice of ½ a lemon

1 cup green beans, cut into ¾-inch pieces
4 vine tomatoes, halved
coconut oil or avocado oil
4 fresh sardines, gutted and cleaned

To make the dressing, marinate the shallots in the red wine vinegar. Meanwhile chop the herbs, peppers and cucumber finely and mix together. Add the olive oil, fish sauce and lemon juice. Drain the shallots and add them to the dressing, discarding the vinegar.

Cook the green beans or runner beans in salted boiling water for 3 to 4 minutes. Drain and rinse in cold water and set aside.

Heat a broiler pan and broil the tomatoes (salted and brushed with avocado or coconut oil) for 3 minutes on each side. Set aside on a serving plate.

Raise the heat to high and broil the whole sardines (salted and brushed with oil) in the same pan for 3 to 5 minutes on each side. Arrange the cooked sardines on the serving plate and drizzle over the dressing. Serve with the beans on the side.

AVOCADO SOUFFLÉ

Enough of the avocado on toast! We all love avocados but they are so much more versatile than you might give them credit for. By now you will know that we shouldn't worry about the fats in avocados: they make us glow and they keep us feeling full. And so, try avocado in a new way—served as a soufflé!

INGREDIENTS

1 ripe Hass avocado, halved and
  pit removed
1 teaspoon blanched (unroasted)
  almond butter, or any other nut butter
4 basil leaves
2 teaspoons pesto (see page 77)
2 egg whites

Preheat the oven to 425°F.

Scoop out the flesh from each half of the avocado, keeping the shells intact. Blend the avocado flesh with the almond butter and basil. Spread a teaspoon of pesto in the base of each shell.

Whip the egg whites until they form soft peaks. Blend a third of this "egg white snow" with the avocado mixture and then slowly and gently fold in the rest without stirring.

Divide the mixture between the hollowed-out shells and cook on a baking sheet in the oven for 7 minutes.

Eat right away!

SPICED SEEDS

As you know, I don't encourage snacking, but if you are going to snack, these seeds are a great staple to have on hand. I like to sprinkle them on salads or over steamed vegetables to give a lovely punch of flavor. Seeds can be so much more than bird food.

INGREDIENTS

2/3 cup pumpkin seeds
3 tablespoons sunflower seeds
3 tablespoons sesame seeds
1 tablespoon fennel seeds
1 tablespoon cumin seeds
½ teaspoon fine sea salt
1 teaspoon olive oil
optional: a sprinkle of smoked paprika
a sprinkle of cayenne pepper

Place a large frying pan over medium-high heat. Once it is hot, put in the pumpkin seeds and keep shaking the pan until you hear some popping and the seeds begin to color. Set them aside in a big bowl.

Toast the sunflower and sesame seeds in the same way, until golden, and add to the pumpkin seeds once done.

Quickly toast the fennel and cumin seeds (this will take less than a minute—don't over-toast them, just heat them until they are fragrant) and add them to the bowl.

Add the salt, oil, smoked paprika (if using) and cayenne pepper to the seeds and mix.

Leave to cool, then put into a sealable jar. These seeds will keep for up to 3 weeks, and are great on salads, roasted or steamed vegetables, or soups.

TUNA TARTARE WITH CRUNCHY AVOCADO

Tuna (part of the mackerel family) is naturally rich in omega-3 essential fatty acids. But I advise you not to eat it more than once a week, due to its mercury content. This is a really refreshing and light dish—buy the best tuna you can find, preferably sustainably sourced.

INGREDIENTS

1 avocado, peeled, halved and pitted
juice of 1 lemon
4 tablespoons macadamia nut oil
a pinch of sea salt
1 bulb of fennel
2 sticks of celery
½ a cucumber, deseeded, skin left on
1 shallot
1 tablespoon salted capers, rinsed
  and chopped
1 teaspoon sesame seeds
½ pound fresh tuna—this needs to be
  sashimi grade, as it is eaten raw

Mash the avocado with the lemon juice. Slowly whisk in the macadamia nut oil and add the sea salt.

Chop the fennel, celery, cucumber and shallot into tiny pieces (you could pulse them in a food processor) and stir into the avocado mixture with the capers.

Toast the sesame seeds for 1 to 2 minutes in a small, hot frying pan until golden.

Chop the tuna finely or put through a meat grinder and arrange on top of the avocado and vegetable mix. Garnish with the toasted sesame seeds.

SALMON BALLS WITH CRUNCHY WHITE SAUCE

A healthier alternative to the standard stodgy fishcake, served with my favorite sauce ever (page 62)!

INGREDIENTS

1 pound skinless salmon fillet, cut into small chunks
1 small zucchini, grated and excess liquid squeezed out
sea salt and freshly ground black pepper
1 tablespoon arrowroot powder
1 egg, preferably free-range or organic, beaten
coconut oil, for greasing

For the sauce:
¾ cup coconut yogurt
1½ tablespoons finely chopped shallots
4 teaspoons finely chopped chives
4 teaspoons finely chopped dill
3 tablespoons finely chopped cucumber, skin on, seeds removed
3 tablespoons fennel, finely chopped
2 tablespoons lemon juice, plus the zest of ½ a lemon
1 tablespoon olive oil
1 level teaspoon sea salt
½ teaspoon toasted and crushed coriander seeds

Preheat the oven to 375°F.

Put the salmon chunks into the food processor and pulse until finely chopped. Add the grated zucchini, salt, pepper and arrowroot and pulse, gradually adding the egg until the mixture binds together.

Roll the mixture into 24 small balls and place them on a lightly greased baking sheet. Bake for 20 to 25 minutes until cooked through and a little golden. (You could fry the balls instead for 4 minutes on each side over medium heat, but they tend to lose their shape and become mini fishcakes.)

Mix all the sauce ingredients together and serve with the salmon balls.

DUCK WITH BEANS AND GREENS

This is a hearty, scrumptious bowl of goodness, perfect for a winter's day. Don't be afraid to try duck if you've never cooked it before: it's incredibly simple and creates the most flavorful dishes because of its natural fat content. Its richness is perfectly complemented by the clean, fresh flavor of fennel.

INGREDIENTS

4 duck legs
1 sweet fennel teabag
a 1-inch piece of fresh ginger, peeled
  and sliced, plus extra to serve
4 cloves of garlic, peeled
1 carrot, sliced in half lengthwise
1 onion, halved and pricked with
  a clove
1 dried chili
1 bay leaf
peel of ½ an orange
1 cup filtered water
2 x 13.5-ounce cans of cannellini beans,
  rinsed and drained
chopped fresh parsley, to garnish
2 bulbs of fennel, halved and blanched
1 bag of lacinato kale, blanched

Preheat the oven to 350°F.

Pan fry the duck legs for 10 minutes, or until golden on both sides. Put the duck legs, teabag, ginger, garlic, carrot, onion, chili, bay leaf, orange peel and water into a cast-iron casserole dish and cook in the oven with the lid on for an hour and a half. Take the lid off and bake for another 30 minutes.

Once cooked, remove and discard the vegetables and flavorings, so that you're left with just the duck and its juices. You can take out the duck legs, shred the meat off the bone and put it back in the stew, or you can leave the legs whole.

Put the casserole dish over medium heat, add the cannellini beans and bring to a boil. Season to taste with salt and pepper, and add some raw ginger at the end for extra spice if you like. Sprinkle with a little chopped fresh parsley.

Serve with blanched fennel and kale.

SIMPLE SARDINE SALAD

Simply and swiftly assembled, this salad is perfect for a hot summer's day. The sharp dressing and salty fish complement each other wonderfully—I'd highly recommend serving this dish to anyone who's not yet a sardine convert.

INGREDIENTS

2 handfuls of cherry tomatoes
olive oil
2 green peppers, deseeded and cut
  into triangles
sea salt and freshly ground black pepper
10 cooked sardine fillets, from a tin
½ cup green olives, pitted and chopped
arugula leaves, or any salad greens
  of your choice

For the dressing:
1 tablespoon lemon juice
2 tablespoons extra virgin olive oil
½ teaspoon Dijon mustard
1 teaspoon chopped fresh parsley

Preheat the oven to 350°F. Put the cherry tomatoes on a baking sheet with 1 tablespoon of olive oil and roast for 10 to 15 minutes.

Fry the green pepper triangles in olive oil for 10 minutes over low heat and season at the end.

Mix the dressing ingredients together and put into a large bowl. Break up the sardines (removing skin and bones if necessary) and add them to the bowl with the peppers, olives, roasted tomatoes and salad leaves. Mix well and serve.

WINTER OXTAIL STEW WITH PUMPKIN AND KALE

What I love about this stew is that all of the nutrients and health-promoting collagen seep out of the oxtail while it slowly cooks, making this dish not only rich in flavor but also incredibly nutritious. Serve with veggies—I love it with parsnip and ginger mash (see opposite) or with a portion of kimchi (see page 84).

INGREDIENTS

2 small onions, finely chopped
2 small carrots, thickly sliced
1½ cups pumpkin, peeled, deseeded and
    cut into ¾-inch cubes
a thumb-sized piece of fresh ginger,
    peeled and finely grated
2 red chilies, deseeded and finely chopped
3 cloves of garlic, finely chopped
2 pounds oxtail pieces, trimmed of any
    excess fat
2 x 13.5-ounce cans of chopped tomatoes
2 cups water
3 tablespoons fish sauce
1 piece of kombu seaweed
1 large handful of kale, stems removed,
    washed and roughly chopped

Mix together the onions, carrots, pumpkin, ginger, chilies and garlic and put them into a slow cooker. Push the oxtail pieces down into the vegetable mixture.

Mix the chopped tomatoes, water and fish sauce together and pour over the oxtail and vegetables, ensuring everything is covered, adding a little extra water if needed.

Add the kombu to the liquid and stew for 5 to 6 hours on a high setting, or 8 to 12 hours on a low setting. Add the kale for the last 5 minutes of cooking time and remove the kombu before serving.

PARSNIP AND GINGER MASH

We tend to limit mashing to just potatoes, but so many starchy vegetables are brilliant when mashed, so get out of your comfort zone and start mashing your greens and other vegetables. This parsnip and ginger one is a staple in my home.

INGREDIENTS

7 large parsnips, peeled and cut into small, equal-sized chunks
a thumb-sized piece of fresh ginger, peeled and sliced
½ cup coconut cream
a pinch of ground ginger
sea salt and freshly ground black pepper
a small handful of fresh parsley, chopped, to serve

Place the parsnips and fresh ginger in a large saucepan of boiling water and cook until tender—this will take roughly 20 minutes.

Drain, and remove as much of the ginger as you can—don't worry if you can't get every slice. Mash the parsnips while slowly pouring in the coconut cream. The consistency should be smooth and fluffy.

Season with a pinch of ground ginger, salt and black pepper to taste. Serve scattered with chopped fresh parsley.

SPICED COCONUT CRÈME ANGLAISE WITH PINEAPPLE AND GOJI BERRIES

Sweet, smooth custard offset by deliciously tangy pineapple is a winning combination. This is a very simple, straightforward recipe which delivers big, fresh flavors—a fantastic alternative to a stodgy pie or crumble.

INGREDIENTS

1 handful of dried goji berries
juice and zest of 1 lemon
1 x 13.5-ounce can of full-fat coconut milk
1 vanilla pod, seeds scraped out
2 thumb-sized pieces of fresh
  turmeric, peeled
2 thumb-sized pieces of fresh
  ginger, peeled
3 egg yolks
⅛ cup raw honey
1 large ripe pineapple

Wash the goji berries in two rinses of water, then leave to soak in the lemon juice for about an hour.

Put the coconut milk and the deseeded vanilla pod into a pan and place over low heat. Bring to a boil, then take the pan off the heat.

Finely grate the turmeric and ginger, then squeeze in a kitchen towel to extract the juice into a large bowl (you can also make turmeric "juice" by adding water to ground turmeric). Add the egg yolks, vanilla seeds and raw honey, then whisk vigorously until smooth and slightly thickened.

Slowly add the coconut milk, whisking continuously, then put the mixture back into the pan and bring slowly to a simmer, continuing to whisk until it has thickened a little more. Remove from the heat, add the lemon zest and leave to cool.

Peel and core the pineapple and cut into ¾-inch chunks. Divide the crème anglaise between four small bowls. Top with the pineapple and drained goji berries.

STAGE ONE / *Chop and blend*

"DON'T STARVE.
DON'T BINGE.
EAT RIGHT, EXERCISE.
YOU WILL GET THERE."

STAGE TWO / *Serve*

GET YOUR GREENS

I didn't want to include a whole section on smoothies, but the following two recipes are favorites of mine for an energy boost. Full of green goodness, they can be drunk at any time of the day. The smoothie is very high in sugar from all of the fruit, so ensure that you eat some protein at the same time to lessen the glycemic response. If you have type 2 diabetes or are trying to lose weight, reduce the amount of fruit in the recipe.

SERVES 2

GREEN SMOOTHIE

INGREDIENTS

1 cup ripe pineapple, peeled and cubed
flesh of 2 large or 3 small passion fruits
3 ounces baby spinach leaves
1 cup coconut water
1 teaspoon coconut oil
½ teaspoon vanilla extract

Make sure the ingredients are at room temperature—if they are too cold, the coconut oil will harden. It's fine to refrigerate the smoothie afterward.

Blend everything in a food processor.

SERVES 3

GREEN MILK

INGREDIENTS

½ cup cashew nuts
2 teaspoons coconut oil
2 cups coconut water
1 small egg yolk or ¼ teaspoon lecithin
¼ pound baby spinach leaves
2 leaves of fresh mint
4 leaves of fresh basil
8 leaves of fresh parsley
¼ teaspoon sea salt
optional: 2–3 dates

The green milk is pure energy in a glass—the perfect way to start your day. Blend everything in a food processor.

STAGE THREE / *Drink*

HAPPY TUMMY

Chapter 7 /
HAPPY TUMMY

———————

Coconut pancakes

Scrambled eggs with roasted tomatoes and dulse

Duck breast with cucumber and orange salad

Individual fish pies

Roasted vegetable soup

Minute steak with roasted fennel and
arugula and caper dressing

Mackerel and rhubarb salad

Baked fish packets

Beef fillet with crunchy broccoli and
eggplant mash

Celeriac ribbons alla carbonara

Beef goulash

Shepherd's pie

Set strawberries with coconut cream

My own journey toward better health began with my gut. As readers of my first book will know, it was my poor digestion that initially prompted me to see a nutritional therapist and eventually become a nutritional therapist myself.

I've found that with clients too it's often their gut that brings them to me in the first place. I truly believe that the health of our gut can have an impact on our entire well-being—from skin conditions to neurological health.

Yet all too often we ignore symptoms, particularly digestive ones. We become out of tune with our bodies and just accept pain, bloating, gassiness or feeling uncomfortably full after eating. It's often only when something gets serious or our symptoms become intolerable that we seek a solution. And most frustratingly with digestive issues, in the absence of a specific diagnosis, there often isn't a straightforward solution.

In my case, I had to take a long hard look at what I was eating: too many sugary, processed foods and too much alcohol—terrible for our gut health because they reduce good gut bacteria and encourage the growth of the harmful kind. (The more healthy bacteria you have thriving in your gut, the more nutrients you will be able to absorb from your food and the better you will look and feel.) The overuse of antibiotics, anti-inflammatories like ibuprofen and hormonal contraceptives also contributed to my issues. I had to begin healing my gut, first by removing the fuel to the fire (changing what I was eating), and then by putting that fire out, which is all about healing, repairing and restoring the gut to its optimal function. It is important first to get checked out by your doctor to ensure that there is nothing sinister causing your symptoms—and certainly do not come off any medication without your doctor's support and guidance.

But how we eat, breathe, move, sleep and think also plays a huge role in our digestive function—stress can inhibit the growth of healthy bacteria in our gut and when we're anxious, angry or thinking negatively we tend to chew and swallow too quickly, which leads to poor digestion. I am forever saying that we don't have teeth in our stomachs! If you suffer with digestive issues, slow down and chew your food properly so that your poor gut doesn't have to try to digest large, unchewed chunks of food.

So what can we do to support our digestive system? Well, first, understanding that we share our bodies with a diverse population of bacteria is key, along with acknowledging that the way that we eat and live influences their behavior. There is much research into this area, looking at how the different strains of bacteria can also influence our behavior, which may explain why some people have different health tendencies: for example, some strains of bacteria can influence us to crave certain foods, others can influence mood. But without the unique knowledge of the different strains and tendencies each of us has, for now, feeding the good bacteria to encourage them to flourish is a good place to start in order to promote the healthiest environment within our digestive systems.

Our gut is often referred to as our second brain. The common sayings "What is your gut telling you?" or "I can feel it in my gut" have arisen because there is a very close interaction between our guts and our brains.[3] Our gut functions can influence how our brain behaves, and vice versa. The gut is involved in the activity of several neurotransmitters, including the feel-good hormones serotonin and dopamine. In fact, studies have found that 95 percent of our serotonin is produced in our gut, so a happy tummy can have a huge impact on your overall levels of happiness and well-being. A lot of our emotions, like fear, happiness and excitement, are "held" and can be felt in our gut, which is why we often have IBS-type symptoms when we're stressed.

All of the recipes in this book are already aimed at being gut-friendly by avoiding gluten, dairy and refined sugar—which I personally have found to be the most crucial food groups to avoid in order to relieve my symptoms and those of my clients—and most are grain-free. But if you are avoiding these foods and still suffering with symptoms, it may be that an extra step is required.

Paying attention to and avoiding high-FODMAP foods could be the next step for you. I urge you to do this with the support of a qualified practitioner, but all of the recipes in this chapter are created using low-FODMAP foods. From my experience, personally and with clients, this is a very individual process which requires you to experiment and see which foods do and don't work for you.

WHAT ARE FODMAPS?

The low-FODMAP diet is a gut-healing way of eating that was developed at the Monash University in Australia in 2005 and has since been used by King's College London and Guy's and St Thomas' Hospitals in London to treat IBS

---

3. http://newsroom.ucla.edu/releases/changing-gut-bacteria-through-245617.

symptoms. FODMAP stands for Fermentable Oligosaccharides, Disaccharides, Monosaccharides and Polyols (phew!). And the high-FODMAP list covers a range of carbohydrates (including some super-healthy ones!) that should be avoided when following the FODMAP plan.

The theory behind the low-FODMAP way of eating is that certain carbohydrates can trigger bacterial fermentation in the gut and by eliminating them from your diet (with guidance from a qualified expert) you can start to reduce your symptoms. If you are suffering from IBS symptoms, I recommend you consult initially with a medical practitioner. If you get diagnosed with IBS then try to follow a low-FODMAP plan, and gradually reintroduce some of the high-FODMAP foods and see which ones trigger the most digestive distress, if any, so that you know which ones to cut out of your diet completely.

The high-FODMAP food list is long and there are many differing versions, so it can seem overwhelming. When I first learned about it I was quite horrified and worried how I could ever suggest a client avoid avocados and apples—two of the foods I consider to be most healthful! But this is the next step to really helping someone to live a life free from the symptoms of IBS.

LOW-FODMAP FOODS:

Broccoli / butternut squash / carrots / celeriac / celery / chilies / zucchini / cucumbers / green peppers / ginger / kale / leeks / lettuces / olives / parsnips / pumpkins / radishes / red peppers / seaweed / spinach / squash / sweet potatoes / bananas / blueberries / grapes / kiwis / lemons / oranges / pineapples / raspberries / strawberries / rhubarb.

HIGH-FODMAP FOODS:

Onions / garlic / cow's milk / yogurt / apples / pears / mangoes / watermelons / peaches / sugar snap peas / Brussels sprouts / cabbages / cereals / legumes / sweeteners ending in "ol" (e.g., sorbitol) / cherries / plums / avocados / cauliflowers / mushrooms.

So with all this in mind, here are some extra-gut-friendly meals . . .

COCONUT PANCAKES

Even people with tummy problems occasionally need a treat now and then, so this recipe is for them. These are *really* good pancakes; they crisp nicely on the outside but are very fluffy and soft on the inside.

INGREDIENTS

¼ cup coconut flour
1½ teaspoons baking soda
a pinch of sea salt
1 teaspoon of vanilla extract
2 medium eggs, preferably free-range
   or organic
½ cup coconut milk
coconut oil
fresh blueberries, coconut flakes
   and maple syrup, to serve

Mix together the dry ingredients in a large bowl. Add the eggs, then slowly add the coconut milk, mixing with a wooden spoon until you get a smooth batter (you might need to add a little more coconut milk, depending on the thickness of your coconut flour—the batter should be quite runny).

Heat a large, non-stick frying pan over medium heat and melt 1 tablespoon of coconut oil. When the oil is hot, spoon in 2 tablespoons of batter for each pancake. You will have to cook them in batches. Leave to fry until completely cooked and brown underneath, then carefully flip over and cook the other side. Transfer the pancakes to a plate and keep them warm while you cook the remaining batter.

Serve in a stack with fresh blueberries, coconut flakes and maple syrup.

Alternatively, press the fresh blueberries into the batter in the pan, so that they're cooked into the pancakes.

Note
You could also use frozen blueberries rather than fresh. Put 2 handfuls and a few tablespoons of water into a small saucepan and bring to a simmer—this gives you lovely, dribbly blueberries with a purple "sauce."

SCRAMBLED EGGS WITH ROASTED TOMATOES AND DULSE

Dulse is a sea vegetable that has a strong flavor; served with eggs it can mimic a nice, crispy smoky bacon. However, dulse is also excellent sprinkled over salads, soups and vegetables. Sea vegetables are rich in minerals, specifically iodine, which can help protect the thyroid.

INGREDIENTS

2 strings of cherry tomatoes, on the vine
extra virgin olive oil
a small handful dulse
coconut oil
4 eggs, preferably free-range or organic
a small handful of fresh chives, chopped
sea salt and freshly ground black pepper

Preheat the oven to 400°F. Drizzle the cherry tomatoes with a teaspoon of extra virgin olive oil and roast in the oven for 10 to 15 minutes.

While the tomatoes are cooking, prepare the dulse. Heat half a tablespoon of coconut oil in a non-stick frying pan and fry the dulse—it'll get slightly soggy at first but will crisp up after a little while. Set aside to drain on a paper towel.

Whisk the eggs together with the chives. Put a little coconut oil or a small splash of olive oil into a non-stick frying pan, and when the oil is warm add the eggs. Stir continuously until cooked through. Season with salt and pepper.

Serve the eggs immediately with the dulse scattered on top and the roasted tomatoes on the side.

DUCK BREAST WITH CUCUMBER AND ORANGE SALAD

Duck is often forgotten about as a great source of protein and it's also rich in good fats. This salad is so special I could have it every single day—it's such a light and satisfying meal to eat.

INGREDIENTS

1 duck breast
5 ounces cucumber
sea salt
1 large orange
1 tablespoon lemon juice
¼ teaspoon grated fresh ginger
4 chive stalks, finely chopped
optional: 1 green chili, finely chopped
  (deseeded if you like)

Score the skin of the duck breast. Put it skin side down in a cold pan and slowly heat up over a low setting. Salt generously. Don't touch it for about 15 to 20 minutes, depending on the size of the breast. The skin will be crisp. Flash-fry the underside of the breast for 1 minute before putting it on to a plate and leaving it to rest for 5 minutes, then cut into slices. (You can cook the duck for longer if you prefer it more well done.)

Meanwhile peel and deseed the cucumber. Cut into triangular chunks (lengthwise), then sprinkle with salt and massage it through. Leave to rest for 20 minutes in the fridge, then rinse and squeeze the cucumber pieces with your hands or a towel.

Peel the orange with a serrated knife and cut out the segments, leaving the pith. Dice the segments, keeping any juice, and add both, along with the lemon juice, grated ginger, chopped chives and chili (if using), to the cucumber and stir well. Serve alongside the duck.

INDIVIDUAL FISH PIES

Many people might not expect to find fish pie in the Happy Tummy section of this book. While I admit it's not as rich as the cream-and-cheese-laden standard fish pie, this is by no means a poor man's version. This is a satisfying, hearty dish that abides by all of the low-FODMAP rules.

INGREDIENTS

1 x 13.5-ounce can of coconut milk
1 tablespoon garlic-infused olive oil
juice and zest of 1 lemon
2 bay leaves
2 x 5-ounce cod fillets
10 ounces undyed smoked haddock
optional: a splash of white wine
sea salt and freshly ground black pepper
1 large celeriac, peeled and chopped into
   equal-sized chunks
2 sprigs of fresh thyme, leaves picked
1½ tablespoons unflavored coconut butter
5 ounces raw jumbo shrimp
3 spring onions, green parts only,
   thinly sliced
a small handful of fresh chives, chopped
1 tablespoon fresh parsley, chopped,
   to serve

Put the coconut milk, garlic oil, lemon juice and zest and bay leaves into a large, deep pan. Add the cod and haddock and bring to a gentle simmer. Poach the fish for approximately 10 minutes until the flesh flakes easily.

Remove the fillets and set aside. Add the wine (if using) to the poaching liquid, season to taste with salt and pepper, and leave to simmer over low heat while you make the celeriac mash.

Preheat the oven to 400°F. Put the celeriac into a pan of boiling water and boil with the thyme leaves until tender. Drain and mash with the coconut butter, and season with salt and pepper.

Flake the fish and divide between four individual ovenproof dishes (or you can use one big dish). Add the jumbo shrimp, spring onions and chives to each pot and pour a quarter of the poaching liquid over them—it should have thickened slightly by now. Top with celeriac mash and bake for 40 to 50 minutes, or until the pies are golden on top.

Scatter with chopped fresh parsley and serve with steamed greens such as broccoli, peas or rainbow chard.

ROASTED VEGETABLE SOUP

I find that roasting the vegetables for this soup gives a wonderful depth of flavor. It can be served without the tapenade (see below for my FODMAP-friendly, garlic-free version), but it really does finish it off beautifully, so it's worth having a look at page 74 and making some especially to go with this. Any leftover tapenade can be kept in the fridge for another day. Eat this soup warm on an autumnal day, or cold, like gazpacho, in the height of summer.

INGREDIENTS

1 red pepper, deseeded and
   roughly chopped
1 zucchini, cut into ½-inch slices
1 eggplant, cut into ½-inch slices
2 sticks of celery, roughly chopped
6 large ripe tomatoes, sliced in half
2 tablespoons olive oil
1 tablespoon balsamic vinegar
1 tablespoon roughly chopped fresh
   thyme leaves
1 tablespoon roughly chopped fresh
   oregano leaves (or 1 teaspoon dried
   oregano)
sea salt and freshly ground black pepper
2½ cups low-FODMAP chicken stock
   (see page 59—must be made without
   onion or garlic)
tapenade (see page 74—must be
   made without garlic; use 1 tablespoon
   garlic-infused olive oil instead) and
   basil leaves, to serve

Preheat the oven to 400°F. Spread the red pepper, zucchini and eggplant in a single layer on a large non-stick baking sheet. Put the celery and the tomatoes (cut side up) on a second non-stick baking sheet. Mix the oil, balsamic vinegar, thyme, oregano and seasoning together and pour over the vegetables on both sheets. Put the sheet with the red pepper, zucchini and eggplant on the top rack of the oven and the sheet with the tomatoes on the rack below. Roast for 25 to 30 minutes, until the vegetables have softened and caramelized.

Let the vegetables cool for a few minutes, then add them to a food processor or blender with half the stock and blend until as smooth as possible. Pour into a clean pan, add the remaining stock and bring to a simmer. Check the seasoning, then serve with a little tapenade on top and a few torn basil leaves scattered over.

MINUTE STEAK WITH ROASTED FENNEL AND ARUGULA AND CAPER DRESSING

A lot of people assume that being healthy means that red meat is off the menu. But I'm delighted to say that it's very much on mine. That said, I am a stickler for ensuring that the meat we eat is of the highest quality and that it is always paired with an abundance of vegetables. Plants are always my main focus, but a little bit of good-quality meat here and there has worked best for me. I have tried being vegan and vegetarian but my health suffered during those phases. We are, after all, omnivores and so, unless you have a specific dislike of, issue with or reaction to meat, I think it's a food group that has an important role in our diet. If you like carpaccio, this recipe also works incredibly well with the beef served raw and very finely sliced.

INGREDIENTS

For the fennel:
1 firm bulb of fennel
olive oil
sea salt and freshly ground
  black pepper
a squeeze of lemon juice

For the dressing:
4 salted anchovies
1 tablespoon capers
1 sun-dried tomato (in olive oil)
1 small clove of garlic, peeled
  and crushed
4 green or Kalamata olives, pitted
1 bag (approx. 2½ ounces) of arugula
1 ripe beefsteak tomato
juice and zest of ½ a lemon
1 tablespoon extra virgin olive oil

For the seared beef:
olive oil
½ pound minute steak
sea salt and freshly ground
  black pepper

Preheat the oven to 350°F. Cut the fennel into thin wedges and place on a baking sheet. Drizzle with olive oil, season, and squeeze over the lemon juice over it. Roast in the oven for 15 to 20 minutes, until softened and lightly charred, turning once during cooking.

Meanwhile, make the dressing by putting all the ingredients (except the olive oil) into a blender and pulsing them a few times. Slowly add the olive oil while you are pulsing, but don't overdo it, as you want to keep some texture. Taste and adjust the seasoning as necessary.

For the beef, heat 1 tablespoon of olive oil in a non-stick frying pan until almost smoking. Season the fillet with salt and pepper and carefully add to the hot pan. Cook for 2 minutes on each side for rare; 3–4 for medium; 4–5 for well done, then transfer to a plate or board, loosely cover with foil and allow to rest for a few minutes.

Arrange the fennel wedges on a serving platter. Slice the beef thinly and place in and around the fennel. Drizzle the arugula dressing over top.

"HAPPINESS
IS THE
HIGHEST FORM
OF HEALTH."

THE DALAI LAMA

MACKEREL AND RHUBARB SALAD

Mackerel is one of my favorite fish—rich in healthy fats. This is an excellent fish to introduce into your diet if you haven't already done so. Many people think of sweet crumble when they think of rhubarb, but here its acidity cuts through the oiliness of this mackerel beautifully—so don't be put off. Give it a try, you won't be disappointed.

INGREDIENTS

½ bulb of fennel
3 tablespoons cider vinegar
2 stalks of rhubarb
juice and zest of 1 orange
2 tablespoons maple syrup
freshly ground black pepper
2 smoked mackerel fillets
2 handfuls of watercress
2 tablespoons walnuts
1 tablespoon extra virgin olive oil

Thinly slice the fennel with a mandolin and put into a bowl. Pour the cider vinegar over it and top up with water until the fennel is just covered. Cover with plastic wrap and rest in the fridge for an hour.

Preheat the oven to 400°F.

Slice the rhubarb into 2-inch pieces and place on a baking sheet. Drizzle 3 tablespoons of the orange juice and all of the maple syrup over the rhubarb and mix. Season with black pepper and roast in the oven for 15 minutes.

Drain the fennel and pat dry on a tea towel. Flake the mackerel fillets and place on a plate with the watercress, rhubarb, fennel and walnuts. Whisk the olive oil with 1 tablespoon of the orange juice and drizzle over the salad. Sprinkle with the orange zest and some black pepper, and serve.

BAKED FISH PACKETS

I used to think this kind of recipe was really difficult to make until I gave it a go. I was so wrong—this is incredibly simple, and such a joy to serve. The smell that hits you when you open up these packets is just fantastic.

INGREDIENTS

2 fillets of white fish, such as cod
  or halibut
a thumb-sized piece of fresh ginger,
  peeled and grated
1 teaspoon garlic-infused olive oil
zest and juice of 1 lime
1 teaspoon coconut aminos, or tamari
½ teaspoon fish sauce
½ cup coconut milk
1 stalk of lemongrass, sliced in half
  lengthwise and bruised
2 kaffir lime leaves, preferably fresh
a handful of fresh cilantro leaves, plus
  2 sprigs and some chopped red chili,
  to serve

Preheat the oven to 400°F.

Cut out two large squares of aluminum foil and place them on a baking sheet. Put a fish fillet in the middle of each, and fold up the sides to create a bowl shape.

Mix together the ginger, garlic olive oil, lime zest and juice, coconut aminos, fish sauce and coconut milk, then pour half over each fillet. Tuck the lemongrass and a lime leaf into each wrapper next to the fish, and sprinkle with the cilantro leaves. Fold up the sides to create a packet, scrunching the top of the foil together so that no liquid or steam can escape.

Bake in the oven for 10 to 15 minutes, or until the fish is cooked through. Garnish each parcel with a sprig of cilantro and a sprinkle of chopped chili and serve with steamed green vegetables, such as bok choy or tenderstem broccoli, or boiled new potatoes if you're not watching your weight.

BEEF FILLET WITH CRUNCHY BROCCOLI AND EGGPLANT MASH

This is my warped version of good old steak and mashed potatoes with an Asian twist. There's nothing like mixing it up!

INGREDIENTS

For the eggplant mash:
1 eggplant
½ a small clove of garlic, peeled and grated
¼ teaspoon peeled and grated ginger
1 level teaspoon toasted sesame oil
1 teaspoon tamari or coconut aminos
sea salt and freshly ground black pepper

For the beef and broccoli:
macadamia nut oil
1 x ½-pound thick fillet (1 inch at least) of beef
sea salt and freshly ground black pepper
1 small head of broccoli, broken into florets (⅓–½ pound)
2 spring onions, trimmed and sliced into pieces ¾ inch thick
toasted sesame seeds, to serve

To make the eggplant mash, cut the eggplant in half lengthwise. Using a sharp knife, score a criss-cross pattern into the flesh, roughly ½ inch apart. Sprinkle each half with a teaspoon of salt and leave to sit for 15 minutes to draw out the moisture. Rinse well under cold water, then steam the eggplant for approximately 15 minutes, until the flesh is soft. Remove from the steamer and, when cool enough to handle, scoop out the flesh into a pan on low heat and add the garlic, ginger, sesame oil and tamari. Heat the mixture for 2 minutes to infuse the flavors. Season well with salt and pepper and mash it all together until smooth using a fork.

Heat a frying pan until very hot, add 1 tablespoon of macadamia nut oil and wait until it gets hot. Season the beef fillet with salt and pepper and fry for 30 seconds on each side, turning and cooking it for 3 minutes total. Remove it from the pan and let it rest.

While the meat is resting, fry the broccoli florets and spring onion slices over medium heat in the same pan, using a teaspoon of macadamia nut oil. Keep stirring and cooking for 3 to 4 minutes (the perfect resting time for the steak in my opinion), adding a tablespoon of water for the last minute of cooking. Slice the steak into strips, serve with the broccoli and eggplant mash and eat immediately!

CELERIAC RIBBONS ALLA CARBONARA

I have never actually eaten a traditional carbonara—just the thought of it makes me feel tired, fat and bloated. But a friend of mine mentioned that it would be their "death row" meal, which made me wonder whether I could make a healthy version that would leave you feeling light. I'm delighted to say I did and, boy, is it good! I still don't want to eat the original version because I'm so happy with mine—I hope you'll all enjoy my twist.

In order to make it, you will need a spiralizer—if you don't have one already, you seriously need to get one! It's not an expensive piece of equipment and it will revolutionize the way you use vegetables.

INGREDIENTS

2 slices of organic smoked Canadian
    bacon
olive oil
2 tablespoons plain coconut yogurt
1 teaspoon lemon juice
1 medium egg yolk, preferably
    free-range or organic
freshly ground black pepper
½ a celeriac (⅓–½ pound), cut into
    ribbons
2 tablespoons finely chopped chives
a pinch of sea salt

Slice the bacon into small pieces. Heat a drizzle of olive oil in a medium frying pan and fry the bacon for 2 to 3 minutes, stirring frequently until golden brown and crisp. Keep an eye on the pan so the pieces don't burn. Remove from the heat and set aside.

In a large bowl, mix the coconut yogurt with the lemon juice, egg yolk and lots of freshly ground black pepper.

Put the celeriac ribbons (the "spaghetti') into a pan of salted boiling water. Wait until the water returns to a boil, then cook for another minute. Drain immediately, pat dry and, while still hot, add the ribbons to the coconut yogurt sauce. Add the bacon, sprinkle with the chives and the sea salt and serve right away.

BEEF GOULASH

When I was first learning about low-FODMAP foods (see pages 218–19), I worried a lot about how I could explain it to my clients and find delicious foods for them to eat. Looking through some really old recipes, I stumbled across a beef goulash and was thrilled when I realized I could make a tummy-friendly version. The beef is meltingly soft, the vegetables hold their shape well and the coconut cream gives a silky texture.

INGREDIENTS

1½ pounds very lean beef, trimmed and cubed
2 tablespoons coconut flour
2 teaspoons smoked paprika
1 teaspoon caraway seeds
coconut oil
5 spring onions, green parts only, cut into 2-inch slices
4 small carrots, scrubbed and cubed
10 ounces celeriac, peeled and cubed
¾ pound cherry tomatoes
2 bay leaves
1½ cups homemade beef or chicken stock
2 tablespoons coconut cream
sea salt and freshly ground black pepper
a handful of fresh cilantro leaves

Mix the beef, coconut flour, paprika and caraway seeds together in a bowl so that all the beef is well coated.

Heat 4 tablespoons of coconut oil in a frying pan and brown the beef a few cubes at a time, making sure not to overcrowd the pan.

Put the browned beef into a slow cooker, then add the spring onions, carrots, celeriac, cherry tomatoes and bay leaves. Pour the stock over them. Don't worry if the liquid doesn't cover all the ingredients—more liquid will be released during cooking.

Cook on a low setting for 4 hours, stirring occasionally. (You can also cook this goulash in a casserole dish—bring everything to a low simmer, then leave covered over the lowest heat for 3 hours, or put it in the oven at 350°F for 3 hours.)

Just before serving, stir the coconut cream through, season to taste with salt and pepper and sprinkle with fresh cilantro.

SHEPHERD'S PIE

There are so many ways to make this British classic, and here's mine. FODMAP-friendly, but just as nourishing and flavorful as you'd expect, this fuss-free dish will warm even the gloomiest winter's evening.

INGREDIENTS

garlic-infused olive oil
1⅓ cups carrots, sliced
½ a stick of celery, diced
2 bay leaves
4 slices of lean, unsmoked Canadian
   bacon, cut into small pieces
1 pound ground lamb
1 x 13.5-ounce can of tomatoes
1 cup chicken stock (see page 59—made
   without garlic, leek or onion)
1 sprig of fresh rosemary
4 sprigs of fresh thyme
sea salt and freshly ground black pepper

For the topping:
2 pounds white potatoes
3 tablespoons unflavored coconut butter
a pinch of ground nutmeg or a grating
   of fresh
optional: grated Parmesan

Heat 2 tablespoons of garlic-infused olive oil in a large, deep frying pan. Add the carrots, celery and bay leaves, and sauté until the celery has softened. Add the bacon and fry until cooked through and lightly golden, then add the ground lamb and fry until the meat has browned. Add the canned tomatoes, stock, rosemary and thyme. Season with salt and pepper. Bring to a boil, then leave to simmer, uncovered, for 30 minutes.

Meanwhile preheat the oven to 400°F.

Next, prepare the topping. Peel the potatoes and cut them into equal-sized chunks, then boil in salted water for 15 minutes or until tender. Mash the cooked potatoes with the coconut butter and nutmeg.

Transfer the lamb mixture to an ovenproof dish and spread the topping evenly over it. Fluff up the potatoes to create small peaks and sprinkle with Parmesan (if using). Bake the pie for 30 minutes, or until the lamb is bubbling around the edges and the potatoes have turned golden. Serve with a leafy green salad.

SET STRAWBERRIES WITH COCONUT CREAM

It's hard to pass up strawberries and cream, but those with digestive health issues might assume they'd have to—not now! You can also make this recipe with any seasonal fruit, such as stewed plums, raspberries, figs or mango.

INGREDIENTS

1 x 13.5-ounce can of coconut milk
2 cups fresh strawberries, stalks removed
2 tablespoons chia seeds
1 teaspoon maple syrup
a pinch of vanilla powder, or 1 teaspoon vanilla extract
a pinch of ground cinnamon
4 fresh strawberries, fresh mint and lemon zest, to serve

Chill the can of coconut milk for at least 2 hours (or overnight) in the fridge, so that the creamy part of the milk floats to the top.

Blend the strawberries into a smooth purée using a food processor, and stir in the chia seeds. Divide the purée between four small ramekins (or two larger ones), cover with plastic wrap and leave to set in the fridge for an hour (or overnight—the fruit will retain its color).

Open the can of coconut milk and scoop out only the creamy top part, leaving the separated liquid. Add the maple syrup, vanilla powder and cinnamon and whip into a light, fluffy cream—be careful not to overwhip.

Spoon the cream into the ramekins and serve garnished with fresh strawberries, lemon zest and mint leaves.

Chapter 8

ENTERTAINING

Chapter 8 /
ENTERTAINING

Cocktails: White wine spritzer / Granny Smith, vodka and matcha cocktail /Cardamom, rose and pink grapefruit gin fizz / Gimlet

Fragrant broth

Millet-sesame croquettes with tamari dipping sauce

Simple shrimp, coconut and eggplant curry

Crunchy vegetable "tabbouleh" with coconut cream and herb dressing

Walnut and sesame "tofu" with spiced amino sauce

Cod with leeks and coconut-oil "hollandaise"

Puy lentil stew with mushrooms, miso and pumpkin

Pork belly with pumpkin and gingered kale

Herby lamb chops with salad

Sweet and savory fruit salad

Coconut yogurt jelly with raspberry and fig compote

Passion fruit "crumble"

One of my favorite ways to cook is for a crowd. We are social animals, and sharing our meals with loved ones is good for the soul. I adore the process of thinking up a recipe I know my friends or family will love, picking out the ingredients, creating the meal and then, finally, sitting down to enjoy it with them.

I like to plan ahead, as I don't enjoy a stifled, stressed dinner party where as the host I'm in the kitchen more than I am enjoying the company. I'd say mine is more the Jamie Oliver–style of cooking, a slightly chaotic, noisy, bustling affair but hopefully with everyone relaxed and enjoying the moment. And that's how I love to entertain—with everything free from fuss and lots of fun. I love to put some music on in my kitchen and have a glass of red wine with my guests while I finish making the food. Sometimes I even get them involved. Children especially love pitching in, so I give them little jobs to do—I think it's important for children to understand where food comes from and how meals are made and I like to help start them early!

In this chapter I'm going to share the recipes I love to make when I'm entertaining. Some of them hardly take any time at all, while others take a bit more effort and are great for when you really want to impress. But they are all delicious and nourishing and will bring a table of people together beautifully.

One thing to remember when you're entertaining is to think about how you want your guests to feel at the end of the night. There's this rather bizarre and age-old tradition of filling our guests so full of food they're barely able to walk away from the table. But it doesn't have to be this way. While my guests are always very well fed, I purposely make meals that leave them feeling light, energized and healthy. Not uncomfortably full and resenting me for weakening their willpower by serving up huge bowls of rich desserts that they are trying to avoid. I think mindfulness extends to entertaining too. I'm not saying don't have fun, but the fun should mostly be about the excellent company and sharing delicious meals, not just about eating enormous amounts of really rich food.

So whether you're cooking for your family, friends or colleagues, here are my all-time favorite crowd-pleasers. Enjoy!

1 / *White wine spritzer*   **2 /** *Granny Smith, vodka and matcha cocktail*

3 / *Cardamom, rose and pink grapefruit gin fizz*   **4 /** *Gimlet*

COCKTAILS

OK, we all know that alcohol does not promote good health. However, let's be realistic, we also know that there are occasions when only alcohol will do. So these are four healthier versions of alcoholic drinks to enjoy in moderation, occasionally.

MAKES 2

WHITE WINE SPRITZER

This is a lighter, zestier approach to that evening glass of wine.

INGREDIENTS

1 lemon
2 teaspoons sea salt
ice
1 cup (8 ounces) dry white wine, such as
  Sauvignon Blanc
club soda

Peel 2 long strips of zest from the lemon and twist them into loops. Finely zest the rest of the lemon peel.

To prepare the wine glasses for serving, mix the finely grated lemon zest and sea salt together and place on a small plate. Dip the rim of each glass into water and then into the lemon and sea salt mixture to create a crust around the edge. Half fill each glass with ice.

Pour the wine into the glasses and top each one with a dash of club soda. Decorate with the lemon peel.

MAKES 2

GRANNY SMITH, VODKA AND MATCHA COCKTAIL

Instead of toxic energy drinks, I suggest you make this goddess of a cocktail. You must use Granny Smith apples for the tanginess, and the matcha will give you healthy wings.

INGREDIENTS

½ teaspoon matcha powder
juice of 6 Granny Smith apples
  (approx. 1 cup)
¼ cup (2 ounces) vodka
1 tablespoon coconut nectar
crushed ice
club soda

Put the matcha powder into a small bowl or jug, add 2 tablespoons of water and whisk together. Transfer to a cocktail shaker, along with the apple juice, vodka and coconut nectar. Shake well, strain into glasses filled with crushed ice and top up each glass with club soda.

CARDAMOM, ROSE AND PINK GRAPEFRUIT GIN FIZZ

I don't remember where I first saw this recipe—somewhere on the Internet a few years ago—but as soon as I did, it was love at first sight. I've been making this cocktail for friends ever since. It's sharp, sour and oh so pretty in pink.

INGREDIENTS

¼ cup (2 ounces) gin
¼ teaspoon rose water
¼ teaspoon ground cardamom
1 cup pink grapefruit juice
juice of 1 lemon
crushed ice
club soda

Place the gin, rose water, ground cardamom, pink grapefruit juice and lemon juice in a cocktail shaker. Shake well, then pour through a fine sieve. Divide between 2 glasses filled with crushed ice and top each up with a splash of club soda.

GIMLET

The gimlet is a classic cocktail that has been around since the early nineteenth century; however, I only discovered it when I was in New York last year. I couldn't believe how simple and clean a drink it is—and perfect for those of you watching your waistlines, due to the low sugar content.

INGREDIENTS

¼ cup (2 ounces) gin
juice of 1 lime
2 teaspoons coconut nectar
crushed ice
2 lime wedges, to serve

Put the gin, lime juice and coconut nectar into a cocktail shaker. Shake well and strain into glasses filled with crushed ice. Serve with the lime wedges.

STAGE ONE / *Preparation*

"NOTHING BRINGS PEOPLE TOGETHER LIKE GOOD FOOD."

STAGE TWO / *Assemble*

STAGE THREE / *Eat*

FRAGRANT BROTH

This light broth is perfect for serving in a large, deep bowl at the table, surrounded by smaller bowls of food to add. That way, everyone can make up their own version.

INGREDIENTS

For the broth:
4 cups light chicken stock
1¼ cups water
2 stalks of lemongrass, bruised
a thumb-sized piece of fresh ginger, peeled and sliced into ¼-inch-thick rounds
juice of 1 lime
2 lime leaves
sea salt and freshly ground black pepper

Flavor options:
2 large chilies (1 red and 1 green), sliced
2 baby bok choy (approx. 1½ ounces), cut in half
1½ ounces baby spinach
¾ cup mushrooms, sliced
¾ ounces snow peas, roughly chopped
½ pound (approx. 2 breasts) poached and shredded chicken breast (see page 48)
5 ounces cooked shrimp (see page 97)
a rainbow of vegetable noodles

To garnish:
cilantro leaves
basil leaves
4 spring onions, trimmed and sliced diagonally
2 tablespoons toasted sesame seeds

To make the broth, put the stock and water into a medium saucepan. Bring to a gentle simmer and add the lemongrass, ginger, lime juice and lime leaves. Simmer over very low heat for 8 to 10 minutes, adjusting the seasoning to taste. Strain into a clean pan.

To serve, present the hot broth at the table with the prepared flavor options in bowls, platters and on boards. Allow everyone to help themselves at the table by putting their chosen ingredients into their own bowls. Ladle the broth over and garnish with the herbs, spring onions and toasted sesame seeds.

MILLET-SESAME CROQUETTES WITH TAMARI DIPPING SAUCE

Millet is a naturally gluten-free grain and therefore a useful ingredient if you occasionally want something bread-like. These are great fun and super simple, but you do need to start them the night before.

INGREDIENTS

For the croquettes:
¾ cup millet grain
sea salt
⅓ cup white sesame seeds
macadamia nut oil

For the dipping sauce:
½ a spring onion
½ a small, mild red chili
2 tablespoons tamari
½ teaspoon sesame oil
2 teaspoons rice vinegar or lime juice

Heat a large frying pan and, when hot, add the millet and shake the pan continuously for 1 to 2 minutes, until the grain is slightly toasted. It should smell fragrant and you will hear it start to pop.

Grind the millet into a flour in a Vitamix or heavy-duty food processor. If you don't have a good blender, use a mortar and pestle. Add ½ cup of hot water and a pinch of salt to the flour, cover and leave at room temperature overnight.

The next day, form the fermented millet paste into a rectangular shape, approximately 4 inches x 5½ inches x ¾ inch, on greaseproof paper. Steam for 45 minutes.

Cut the steamed millet paste into croquettes approximately 3 inches x ¼ inch and roll in the white sesame seeds. Fry in 2 tablespoons of macadamia nut oil for 5 minutes on each side, until golden, crispy and heated through. Drain on paper towels.

To make the tamari dipping sauce, chop the spring onion and chili very finely and stir in the rest of the ingredients.

SIMPLE SHRIMP, COCONUT AND EGGPLANT CURRY

Many of us love a curry, and this is my absolute favorite. It's rich in flavor but won't leave you in that post-curry slump. I love this because it's so simple and everything's made in one pot—perfect to share or enjoy alone, and I don't think it needs any rice!

INGREDIENTS

coconut oil
1 onion, chopped
2 cloves of garlic, finely grated
a thumb-sized piece of fresh ginger, peeled and grated
1 red or green chili, deseeded (if you like) and finely chopped
1 teaspoon ground cumin
1 teaspoon ground coriander
½ teaspoon garam masala
½ teaspoon turmeric
sea salt and freshly ground black pepper
1 eggplant, grated or finely sliced
¼ pound cherry tomatoes, cut in half
1¼ cups vegetable stock
1 cup coconut milk
½ pound raw tiger shrimp, peeled
a large handful of baby spinach

Heat 1 tablespoon coconut oil in a large sauté pan and fry the onion, garlic, ginger and chili for 2 to 3 minutes to soften, stirring frequently. Stir in the spices and season well with a pinch of salt and pepper. Continue to fry over medium heat for a further minute or two until fragrant. Transfer the mixture to a mini food processor and blend until smooth, adding a splash of water if necessary to loosen the consistency to a paste.

Return the pan to the heat and put in another tablespoon of coconut oil. Add the paste and fry for 2 to 3 minutes. Add the eggplant and sauté for a minute or two, stirring to coat it with the paste, before adding the cherry tomatoes. Pour in the stock, bring to a boil, then reduce the heat and simmer gently for 10 to 12 minutes.

Add the coconut milk and the shrimp and cook for 3 to 4 minutes, until the shrimp are pink and cooked through and the sauce has just thickened. Stir in the spinach, wilt for a minute, then season to taste with salt and pepper. Serve immediately.

CRUNCHY VEGETABLE "TABBOULEH" WITH COCONUT CREAM AND HERB DRESSING

I'm not sure how this recipe came about. I think it was a mix of leftovers in my fridge, but somehow it just works. The creaminess of the coconut cream with the crunch of the vegetables and the sharpness of the pesto is really unusual, and a perfect start to a dinner party.

INGREDIENTS

For the dressing:
1 x 13.5-ounce can of coconut milk
2 tablespoons coconut oil
½ teaspoon sea salt flakes
½ bunch of fresh parsley
½ bunch of fresh basil
2 sprigs of fresh tarragon
2 sprigs of fresh mint
1 clove of garlic
juice of 1 lemon
½ cup extra virgin olive oil

For the "tabbouleh":
6 spears of green asparagus, woody
  ends snapped off
3 spring onions, trimmed
1 cucumber (approx. ¾ pound), skin on
1 bulb of fennel (approx. ½ pound)
1 gem lettuce
1 carrot, peeled
juice of 1 lemon
½ cup toasted pine nuts

Drain off the liquid coconut milk and place the remaining solids in a large bowl. Melt 2 tablespoons of coconut oil in a saucepan over a gentle heat. Once cooled, add to the coconut milk solids along with the salt. Whip until creamy in texture.

Pulse the herbs, garlic and lemon juice together in a food processor. With the motor still running, gradually add the olive oil. Add this pesto to the coconut cream and stir through.

To make the "tabbouleh," finely chop all the vegetables, then squeeze the lemon juice over the top. Mix in the dressing and serve in ramekins. Garnish with the toasted pine nuts.

WALNUT AND SESAME "TOFU" WITH SPICED AMINO SAUCE

This is not truly tofu, as it's not made with any soy product. Instead the base mixture is made by whisking kudzu powder (which comes from a Japanese plant and is wonderful for relieving hangovers!) with chicken stock and tahini. A strange combination, you might be thinking, but it gives a delicious, creamy, firm result which does resemble tofu. The baked walnuts scattered on top give a fantastic crunch to contrast with the smooth texture of the "tofu," and the spicy amino sauce finishes the dish off with a chili hit. I serve this as a simple starter, or you can break it up and serve with salads or vegetables, just as you would with regular tofu.

INGREDIENTS

½ cup walnut halves
1 teaspoon toasted sesame oil
1 teaspoon sea salt
2 cups chicken stock
½ cup kudzu powder
⅓ cup tahini
1 teaspoon ground cumin

For the sauce:
4 tablespoons coconut aminos
   or tamari
1 spring onion, chopped
3 thumb-sized pieces of fresh
   ginger, grated
2 teaspoons sesame oil
10 drops of Tabasco

Bake the walnut halves at 350°F for 8 minutes. Rub them in a tea towel to remove as much skin as possible, then chop. Put them into a bowl with the sesame oil and salt, mix well and set aside.

Add a little of the stock to the kudzu powder and whisk to form a smooth paste. Pour into a medium saucepan, add the rest of the stock and place the pan over medium heat. Add the tahini and cumin, and whisk continuously as you would Béchamel sauce. It will thicken quite suddenly, so be careful—whisk until it's the consistency of a thick pudding, then take it off the heat.

Wet the inside of a square container (such as a glass baking dish)—this will be your mold. Pour in the thick mixture and smooth it out on top. Tap the container gently a few times to get rid of any air bubbles and scatter the walnuts evenly on top.

Leave to cool, then cover and put in the fridge for 2 hours. Meanwhile, combine all the sauce ingredients, mix well and set aside.

Place a plate over the container and turn swiftly upside down, then gently remove the container. Cut the "tofu" carefully into slices and serve chilled with the amino sauce and a green salad.

COD WITH LEEKS AND COCONUT-OIL "HOLLANDAISE"

This dish works well with any white meaty fish—get the best sustainable fish available to you. This "hollandaise" isn't really a hollandaise, so don't expect the same behavior (if you're used to making the traditional version). However, the method is slightly similar, so that's how it got its name. Ultimately this is a creamy, delicious and very easy-to-make sauce, and I absolutely love it with this simple steamed cod.

INGREDIENTS

For the "hollandaise":
4 egg yolks, preferably free-range
   or organic
½ teaspoon Dijon mustard
½ cup light vegetable or fish stock,
   or water
½ teaspoon mild curry powder
2 tablespoons melted coconut oil
1 teaspoon lemon juice
zest of ½ a lemon

For the cod and leeks:
2 leeks, washed and trimmed,
   sliced into 1-inch pieces
sea salt
4 x ⅓-pound cod fillets

Heat a medium-size glass bowl over a saucepan of barely simmering water. Add the egg yolks, mustard, stock and curry powder to the bowl and whisk continuously over the heat for a few minutes, until the mixture starts to thicken. Then slowly add the melted coconut oil and keep whisking until you have your "hollandaise" sauce. It should coat the back of a spoon and be of pouring consistency. Remove from the heat and whisk in the lemon juice and zest. This will slightly thicken the mixture further.

Blanch the leeks in salted boiling water for 6 minutes, then drain and rinse them under cold water.

While the leeks are cooking, heat about an inch of water in a saucepan and fit a steamer on top. Place the cod fillets in the steamer, cover with a lid and steam for 8 to 10 minutes, depending on their size. Add the leeks to the fish for the last 2 to 3 minutes of steaming.

Arrange the cod and leeks on serving plates and spoon over plenty of the "hollandaise" sauce.

"IF IT'S IMPORTANT
TO YOU, YOU'LL
FIND A WAY. IF IT'S
NOT, YOU'LL FIND
AN EXCUSE."

PUY LENTIL STEW WITH MUSHROOMS, MISO AND PUMPKIN

This is a hearty stew to warm you up on a cold day. Lentils are a source of protein, so essential in a vegetarian or vegan diet. Just replace the chicken stock with vegetable stock to make this a vegetarian or vegan dish. Use any pumpkin if you can't source green.

INGREDIENTS

1¼ cups Puy lentils
8 dried shiitake mushrooms
½ an onion, peeled
1 clove of garlic, peeled
a 4-inch piece of kombu seaweed
1 cup chicken stock
2 teaspoons tamari
1 tablespoon deodorized coconut butter
2 ounces precooked, vacuum-packed
  chestnuts
1 cup green pumpkin, skin on, seeds
  removed, cut into ¾-inch cubes
a thumb-sized piece of fresh ginger,
  finely grated
1 tablespoon brown rice miso

Cover the lentils with water and soak overnight. Soak the shiitake mushrooms in 1½ cups of hot water, ideally overnight also.

Drain and rinse the lentils. Put them into a pan with the onion, garlic, the shiitake mushrooms and their soaking water, and the kombu seaweed. Add an additional ¾ cup of water if the lentils aren't quite covered.

Bring to a boil, cover and reduce the heat to a gentle simmer. Cook for 30 minutes, then remove and discard the garlic and kombu.

Add the chicken stock, tamari, deodorized coconut butter, chestnuts, green pumpkin and grated ginger. Make sure that the vegetables are covered by the stock (add water, if necessary). Add the brown rice miso, cover the pan and cook over medium heat for another 15 minutes.

PORK BELLY WITH PUMPKIN AND GINGERED KALE

A relatively cheap cut of meat, yet full of flavor and so easy to prepare, pork belly is a great alternative to Sunday's roast beef. Pumpkin—king of the squash, in my opinion—is a wonderful addition to this hearty meal.

INGREDIENTS

1¾ pounds pork belly
2 cups chicken stock
a thumb-sized piece of fresh ginger, peeled and cut in half lengthwise
1 bunch of spring onions, trimmed and left whole
2 star anise
4 tablespoons tamari
1 small green pumpkin
olive oil
sea salt and freshly ground black pepper
1 red pepper, chopped
¼ teaspoon ground coriander
a thumb-sized piece of fresh ginger, peeled and grated
1 x ½-pound bag of kale
apple cider vinegar, to taste

Preheat the oven to 400°F.

Put the pork belly into a casserole dish, skin side up, and add the stock, ginger, spring onions, star anise and tamari. Bring to a boil on the stovetop, then cover and cook in the oven for 2 hours.

Once the pork's been in the oven for 1 hour, prepare the pumpkin. Halve and deseed it, then cut into bite-size chunks. Place the chunks on a baking sheet, drizzle with 2 tablespoons of olive oil and season with salt and pepper. Roast in the oven for the remainder of the pork's cooking time (about 40 minutes).

Take the casserole dish out of the oven, remove the pork, slice and set aside to rest. Remove and discard the solid stock ingredients and put the casserole dish over low heat. Add the chopped red pepper, ground coriander and ginger to the sauce, then add the kale and cover with a lid. Simmer for five minutes, or until the kale is tender but still has bite.

Adjust the seasoning with salt, pepper and apple cider vinegar, and serve with the sliced pork belly and roast pumpkin.

HERBY LAMB CHOPS WITH SALAD

Lamb chops only require a few minutes to cook, so they are a regular evening meal in my house and I love to serve them when friends come over for a casual supper. There are lots of elaborate recipes available but I keep mine simple: grilled and served with a lovely fresh herby green salad.

INGREDIENTS

8 x thick loin lamb chops
2 sprigs of fresh rosemary, leaves
   picked and finely chopped
4 sprigs of fresh thyme, leaves
   picked and finely chopped
2 sprigs of fresh oregano, leaves
   picked and finely chopped
6 cloves of garlic, finely chopped
4 tablespoons olive oil
sea salt and freshly ground
   black pepper

For the salad:
1 x ¼-pound bag of green salad leaves
1 tablespoon finely chopped chives
½ a small bunch of fresh basil or mint,
   leaves picked and roughly chopped
1 large avocado, pitted, peeled
   and sliced
½ a cucumber, halved, deseeded
   and sliced

For the dressing:
3 tablespoons extra virgin olive oil
1 tablespoon red wine vinegar

Put the lamb chops into a big bowl. Mix the rosemary, thyme, oregano leaves and garlic into the olive oil, pour this marinade over the lamb and toss. (You can do this the day before, then cover the bowl with plastic wrap and keep it in the fridge.)

When you are ready to cook, heat the broiler to medium high. Season the lamb chops well, then put them on a broiler pan lined with foil. Broil for 5 minutes on each side, until they are golden on the outside but still slightly pink in the middle. If you prefer your chops well done, broil them for slightly longer. Put the chops on a warmed plate, wrap in foil and leave to rest for 10 minutes.

While the chops are resting, prepare your green salad. Arrange the salad leaves on a large platter, sprinkle the herbs over them, then top with the avocado and cucumber slices. Whisk the olive oil and red wine vinegar together with seasoning, then drizzle this over the salad just before serving with the lamb chops.

SWEET AND SAVORY FRUIT SALAD

I don't have much of a sweet tooth these days and don't often eat any kind of dessert. However, many people do, so this recipe meets both of our needs: a little bit of savory with an interesting twist on a boring fruit salad. Don't knock it until you've tried it!

INGREDIENTS

For the dressing:
2 tablespoons raw honey
4 tablespoons extra virgin olive oil
juice of ½ a lime

For the salad:
1 small pineapple, peeled and cored,
  cut into quarters
1 Granny Smith apple, cored and sliced
  thinly on a mandolin
½ a cucumber, peeled into strips using
  a peeler or mandolin
6 strawberries, sliced
sea salt and freshly ground
  black pepper
a sprig of fresh mint

To make the dressing, blend the honey, olive oil and lime juice together in a small bowl.

Put the pineapple, Granny Smith apple, cucumber ribbons and strawberry slices into a large bowl and toss together.

Pour the dressing over at the last minute before sprinkling with salt and pepper. Scatter a few baby mint leaves over the top and serve immediately.

COCONUT YOGURT JELLY WITH RASPBERRY AND FIG COMPOTE

This is my take on pannacotta—the marriage of coconut yogurt with gelatin couldn't be simpler. I encourage you to play around with different fruits, although I'm very partial to this raspberry and fig combination. It looks so pretty, and I'm sure your guests will be impressed.

INGREDIENTS

For the compote:
4 fresh figs
4 dried figs, soaked overnight, then rinsed
¾ cup raspberries
½ teaspoon vanilla essence or
   seeds from ½ a vanilla pod
6 fresh mint leaves

6 leaves of gelatin
2 cups coconut yogurt
chopped Brazil nuts, cacao nibs
   and baby mint leaves, to serve

Blend the fresh figs with the soaked dried figs, raspberries, vanilla essence or seeds and the mint leaves until smooth, slightly thickened but still of dropping consistency. Add some soaking water if needed. Divide this mixture between four parfait glasses or small tumblers.

Soak the gelatin leaves in water for 10 minutes. Once softened, heat them with 4 tablespoons of water until dissolved; add this to the coconut yogurt and whisk the mixture until well incorporated. Pour on top of the fig mixture and place in the fridge to cool.

Just before serving, sprinkle with chopped Brazil nuts, raw cacao nibs and baby mint leaves.

PASSION FRUIT "CRUMBLE"

This is such a sweet little dessert. As you know, I'm not one for sweet treats but this is a little pop of yumminess—perfect for dinner parties, and it won't leave your guests rolling around on the floor with indigestion.

INGREDIENTS

1 cup raspberries
1 teaspoon coconut oil
1 vanilla pod, cut in half and seeds scraped out
1 tablespoon coconut blossom nectar or maple syrup (or sweetener of your choice)
1 small eating apple, peeled and cored
3 large passion fruits
¼ cup cashew nuts, finely chopped
2 teaspoons coconut sugar
6 mint leaves, finely chopped

Preheat the oven to 350°F.

In a saucepan over low heat, cook the raspberries with the coconut oil, vanilla seeds and pod, and the coconut blossom nectar or maple syrup for 3 to 4 minutes, until the berries have softened. Pulse the apple in a food processor, add to the compote and cook for another minute. Take off the heat and remove the vanilla pod.

Halve and empty the passion fruits, reserving the shells, and put into a bowl with the compote. If the compote is very runny, strain the juices through a sieve into the saucepan and bubble over medium heat until thick and syrupy. Pour this syrup back into the compote. If it's slightly too tart for your taste, add a little more coconut blossom nectar or maple syrup.

Spoon the compote into the passion fruit shells, sprinkle with the chopped cashews and a little coconut sugar. Bake for 20 to 30 minutes (depending on your oven). Serve sprinkled with the finely chopped mint.

Chapter 9

EVERYDAY FOOD

Chapter 9 /
EVERYDAY FOOD

Baked sweet potatoes with coconut-yogurt dressing
and spiced pine nuts

Baked chicken meatballs with almond sauce

Sun-dried tomato and harissa turkey burgers

Homemade baked beans

Butternut squash "pasta" with sage and pine nuts

Vegetarian chili with cauliflower rice

Crispy, spicy chicken drumsticks with fragrant coleslaw

Green burgers with green sauce

Spiced winter stew with orange blossom water, apple and lime

Quick tuna omelet

Chicken and tarragon casserole

Spiced roast chicken

Spicy parsnip chips

Herby zucchini fries

Fish sticks with fava beans

I got the idea for this chapter after constantly being asked by clients and sticks on social media for healthy versions of their favorite everyday foods like fish sticks, fried chicken and baked beans.

Initially I didn't like the idea of providing this sort of recipes because I don't think we should look to or rely on "comfort" foods such as these. I have worked with so many clients with "dysfunctional eating," who believe that food is all they have to look forward to, the only positive and good thing in their lives. They eat when they're feeling stressed, bored, unhappy, lonely or sad. It is true that our brains do release opioids when we eat sugars and fats, so that we get a soothing, comforting feeling from eating those foods, but it is always temporary. And breaking that cycle can be just as hard as kicking any other addiction. For many, eating habits are really unconscious and they just don't know why they continue to eat even when they are full. Many of us seek comfort from food, despite knowing deep down that food won't make a long-lasting change in our emotional state.

So much of my work is about educating clients to become more aware, more conscious of their habits and to accept that the only time they need to eat is when they feel hungry and need nourishment. While I absolutely love food and get a lot of pleasure from it, I don't turn to it to make me feel happy. So take pleasure from food, of course, but don't use it to fix negative emotions. And if you feel that you are trapped in a cycle of comfort eating, take heart from the fact that you can overcome it. Eating mindfully and with grace, knowing what you're going to eat in advance, and sitting down to share meals with loved ones will help you break the cycle. You may have to endure a little discomfort at first, while you create new, more positive habits. Remember to feed hunger, not emotions.

I don't want you to make the food in this chapter to cheer yourself up, because no food can do that. Rather, see these dishes as delicious everyday foods you can quickly throw together when you fancy something warm and familiar. These recipes are also good for people who have been eating a lot of pre-prepared, canned or frozen versions and are trying to wean themselves on to more nourishing, fresher alternatives.

Either way, I hope you love these recipes as much as I do!

BAKED SWEET POTATOES WITH COCONUT-YOGURT DRESSING AND SPICED PINE NUTS

Sweet potatoes are such a delicious and nourishing addition to our diets. They contain vitamins A and C, B vitamins and potassium, and are a great source of fiber. However, from a sugar perspective, they are no different from the humble white potato. And so, if you're trying to lose weight, keep sweet potato consumption occasional, not daily.

INGREDIENTS

4 sweet potatoes
¼ cup pine nuts
¼ teaspoon sea salt
a pinch of smoked paprika

For the dressing:
½ a clove of garlic
sea salt
1 cup coconut yogurt
2 tablespoons olive oil
zest and juice of ½ a lemon
½ tablespoon chopped chives
freshly ground black pepper

Preheat the oven to 350°F.

Prick the sweet potatoes all over with a fork and bake in their skins for about 40 minutes on the top shelf of the oven, until they are soft. Set aside until cool enough to handle.

Meanwhile, make the dressing. Crush the garlic with a pinch of sea salt using a mortar and pestle. Mix in the coconut yogurt, olive oil, lemon zest and juice, the chopped chives and some pepper.

Just before serving, heat a pan until very hot. Add the pine nuts and keep shaking the pan until the nuts are evenly colored. Add the salt and the smoked paprika and shake the pan once more before transferring the nuts to a plate. Be careful not to let them burn—this can happen very quickly.

To serve, spoon the dressing over the potatoes and sprinkle with the pine nuts and any leftover chopped chives.

BAKED CHICKEN MEATBALLS

This dish tastes a lot naughtier than it actually is. It's ideal for sharing with friends, and leftovers, if there are any, are perfect for lunch the next day. Although it works well with quinoa, I prefer it just with plenty of greens.

INGREDIENTS

For the almond sauce:
¾ cup chicken stock
1 tablespoon dried mushroom powder
7 tablespoons almond butter

For the meatballs:
½ pound button mushrooms
3 leeks
olive oil
sea salt and freshly ground black pepper
2 x 5-ounce skinless chicken breasts, cut into strips and pulsed in a food processor
1 egg yolk
½ tablespoon finely chopped chives

For the quinoa:
1 cup quinoa (presoaked in warm water overnight is best)
1 tablespoon olive oil
1 tablespoon almond butter

To make the almond sauce, bring the chicken stock and the mushroom powder to a boil, then remove from the heat. One tablespoon at a time, pour this mixture into a bowl of almond butter and stir until you have the consistency of single cream. Set aside.

Preheat your oven to 400°F.

Shred the mushrooms and the green parts of the two leeks, keeping the white parts for later. Fry in 1 teaspoon of olive oil on high heat for 10 minutes, adding a pinch of salt and stirring until the excess liquid reduces.

Meanwhile, put the quinoa in a pan with 1 cup cold water and bring to a boil, then cover and lower the heat. Cook gently for 5 to 10 minutes, until the water is absorbed. Turn off the heat and leave to rest for 10 minutes. Then add a pinch of salt, the olive oil and the almond butter and mix well.

To make the meatballs, combine the chopped chicken with the egg yolk, chives, and the cooled mushroom-leek mixture in a large bowl. Season with salt and pepper and mix well. Roll the mixture into tablespoon-sized balls and place on a large baking sheet lined with foil. Bake for 10 to 15 minutes until just cooked and soft—do not let them overcook.

While the meatballs are cooking, chop the white part of the first two leeks and the whole third leek into ¾-inch slices. Cook in boiling water for 7 minutes, until softened, then drain and add to the quinoa. Gently warm the almond sauce. To serve, top the quinoa with the chicken meatballs and drizzle with the almond sauce.

SUN-DRIED TOMATO AND HARISSA TURKEY BURGERS

Burgers have such a bad rap, but actually they can be a really healthy option (minus the large portion of gluten!). Super-easy to make and brilliant for batch cooking, these are a favorite of mine that I've been making for years. Wrap the burger in some nice crunchy lettuce with a dollop of mustard on top and I promise that you won't miss that bun.

INGREDIENTS

For the burgers:
1 pound ground turkey
2 shallots, finely chopped
1 clove of garlic, finely chopped
4 tablespoons chopped fresh herbs,
  such as parsley or cilantro
6 sun-dried tomatoes, finely chopped
1 egg yolk
2 teaspoons harissa paste
sea salt and freshly ground black pepper
coconut oil

To serve:
1 gem lettuce, leaves separated
1 avocado, peeled, pitted and cut
  into slices
2 vine tomatoes, sliced
Dijon mustard

Mix the ground turkey, shallots, garlic, herbs, sun-dried tomatoes and egg yolk together in a large bowl. Add the harissa paste, season well with salt and pepper and mix again.

Using your hands, divide the mixture into four and press into patties, roughly 1 inch thick. Place on a plate, cover with plastic wrap and refrigerate for 30 minutes.

When you are ready, preheat the oven to 400°F.

Remove the burgers from the fridge and lightly grease a non-stick baking sheet with a touch of coconut oil. Arrange the burgers on the sheet and bake in the oven for 20 to 25 minutes, turning once halfway through cooking.

Serve the burgers on a bed of the lettuce leaves with the sliced avocado and tomato on top of each one. These are particularly lovely with a dollop of Dijon mustard.

HOMEMADE BAKED BEANS

So much tastier than their canned alternative, my homemade baked beans are a simple, nutritious take on a pantry staple. This recipe delivers a rich, silky tomato sauce while allowing the beans to retain their structure.

INGREDIENTS

olive oil
2 stalks of celery, finely chopped
1 large carrot, peeled and finely chopped
1 clove of garlic, finely chopped
1 dried chipotle chili
sea salt and freshly ground black pepper
1½ pounds fresh tomatoes, roughly
   chopped
3 tablespoons tomato purée
1 teaspoon paprika
1 tablespoon Worcestershire sauce
2 x 13.5-ounce cans of navy beans,
   drained and rinsed
a little chopped fresh parsley and a few
   lemon wedges, to serve

Heat 1 tablespoon of olive oil in a saucepan and sweat the celery, carrot, garlic and chili until the vegetables are softened. Remove the chili and season with salt and pepper.

Add the tomatoes, tomato purée, paprika and Worcestershire sauce, then cover the pan and simmer over low heat for 25 minutes. Add a splash of water as it cooks, to loosen the sauce.

Add the navy beans, cover and heat through gently, then season to taste. Serve with the fresh parsley and sliced lemon wedges.

BUTTERNUT SQUASH "PASTA" WITH SAGE AND PINE NUTS

The classic Italian flavor pairing of butternut squash, sage and pine nuts works so well here, without the need for pasta to bring it all together. The squash becomes your "pasta"!

INGREDIENTS

extra virgin olive oil
1 clove of garlic, finely chopped
a large handful of fresh sage leaves
1 small butternut squash, peeled, deseeded and spiralized
sea salt and freshly ground black pepper
2 tablespoons toasted pine nuts
a squeeze of lemon juice

Heat 2 tablespoons of extra virgin olive oil in a large sauté pan, add the garlic and sage and fry over low heat for 1 minute. Set aside in a bowl.

Put the spiralized butternut squash into the same pan with a little more oil. Season well and sauté over medium heat for 2 to 3 minutes. Stir in the garlic-sage mixture and the toasted pine nuts.

Add a splash of water to help steam the squash and cook for another 2 minutes or until it is just tender. Squeeze a little lemon juice over, drizzle over a little more extra virgin olive oil and sprinkle with a pinch of salt and pepper.

"IF IT CAME FROM
A PLANT, EAT IT,
IF IT WAS MADE IN
A PLANT, DON'T."

MICHAEL POLLAN

VEGETARIAN CHILI WITH CAULIFLOWER RICE

Traditional chili is made with ground beef and served with lots of rice, but I see no reason why we can't steal the flavors, add more plants, remove the starch and still enjoy a wholesome, hearty, delicious dish. For those of you who do feel the need for rice, I encourage you to substitute this cauliflower version for the real thing—so simple, but many will be fooled.

INGREDIENTS

olive oil
1 onion, finely chopped
2 cloves of garlic, finely chopped
   or grated
1 red chili, finely chopped
   (deseeded if you like)
1 carrot, peeled and grated
1 zucchini, peeled and grated
1 teaspoon ground turmeric
2 teaspoons ground coriander
2 teaspoons ground cumin
1 teaspoon ground cinnamon
2 tablespoons tomato purée
½ pound cherry tomatoes, cut in half
1¾ cups vegetable stock, or water
1 large cauliflower
1 x 13.5-ounce can of kidney beans,
   chickpeas or cannellini beans
sea salt and freshly ground black pepper
a handful of fresh cilantro leaves, to serve

Heat 2 tablespoons of oil in a large sauté pan and fry the onion, garlic and chili for 2 to 3 minutes over medium-low heat until softened. Add the grated carrot and zucchini and sauté for an additional 2 minutes. Add the spices and cook gently for another 1 to 2 minutes.

Stir in the tomato purée and heat through for a minute before adding the cherry tomatoes. Pour in the vegetable stock, bring to a boil, then reduce the heat to a simmer. Cook for 15 to 20 minutes to reduce and thicken the sauce, stirring frequently.

While the chili is reducing, make the cauliflower rice by pulsing the florets in a food processor or blender until they reach the texture of rice. To cook, steam in a shallow pan of water for 3 to 4 minutes.

When the chili has reduced, add the beans or chickpeas, season to taste with salt and pepper and cook for another 5 minutes.

Garnish with the fresh cilantro leaves and serve with the cauliflower rice.

CRISPY, SPICY CHICKEN DRUMSTICKS WITH FRAGRANT COLESLAW

This is another recipe I created for Sam Smith, who has a bit of a penchant for Kentucky Fried Chicken, so in order to help him stay as healthy as possible, I created this version and it got the thumbs up from him. It's crunchy on the outside, juicy on the inside and full of flavor: exactly what you want from fried chicken.

INGREDIENTS

8 chicken drumsticks
coconut oil
lemon wedges, to serve

For the brine:
½ cup sea salt
¼ cup coconut blossom nectar
4 cups lukewarm water

For the spicy crust:
1 cup red lentils
1 tablespoon ground turmeric
1 teaspoon ground cumin
1 teaspoon ground coriander seeds
1 teaspoon cayenne powder
1 teaspoon dried thyme leaves
1 egg, preferably free-range or
   organic, beaten

For the coleslaw:
½ white cabbage, shredded
2 carrots, shredded
2 spring onions, finely chopped
1 tablespoon toasted fennel seeds
1 tablespoon toasted sesame seeds
2 egg yolks
lemon juice and zest, to taste
½ cup macadamia nut oil
¾ cup extra virgin olive/sunflower/
   walnut oil
sea salt and freshly ground black pepper

Mix the brine ingredients together until the salt and coconut blossom nectar have dissolved. Pour over the chicken, cover and store in the fridge for 2 hours or overnight.

Grind the lentils to a flour in a food processor, then mix in the spices and thyme and set aside, sealed to keep in the flavors.

While the chicken is brining, prepare the coleslaw. Mix the vegetables and seeds together in a large bowl, then make the mayonnaise. Whisk together the egg yolks and lemon zest, then slowly add first the macadamia nut oil and then the rest of the oil, whisking as you go, until you get a thick, silky consistency. Squeeze in the lemon juice and season to taste. Mix well, cover and rest in the fridge until ready to serve.

Remove the chicken from the brine and steam for 15 to 20 minutes or until cooked through. Pat dry with kitchen towel. Roll each drumstick in the beaten egg and then in the spice mix, until completely covered.

Heat 2 tablespoons of coconut oil in a large frying pan until very hot, then fry the drumsticks (in two batches) for 6 to 8 minutes, until each side is browned—you may need to add more coconut oil for the second batch if the pan is looking dry. Serve with the coleslaw and a wedge of lemon.

GREEN BURGERS WITH GREEN SAUCE

Green is my favorite color and greens are my favorite foods, so wherever I can I try to eat them in as many different, creative ways as possible. These green burgers are surprisingly filling and utterly tasty—so go green!

INGREDIENTS

For the green sauce:
¾ cup coconut yogurt
1 teaspoon salted capers
1 salted anchovy
zest and juice of 1 large lemon
2 tablespoons olive oil
a small bunch of fresh chives
a small bunch of fresh parsley
a small bunch of fresh mint

For the burgers:
¾ cup frozen baby peas
¾ cup frozen baby fava beans
3 ounces fresh spinach
a small bunch of fresh basil
a small bunch of fresh parsley
½ pound small cooked shrimp
1 heaping tablespoon arrowroot powder
½ teaspoon ground coriander
1 teaspoon sea salt
1 large egg, preferably free-range
  or organic, beaten
coconut oil

To make the green sauce, blend all the ingredients roughly in a food processor. For the burgers, blanch the baby peas and baby fava beans in salted boiling water for 2 to 3 minutes, then scoop out and put into iced water. Once cold, drain and set aside.

Blanch the spinach, basil and parsley together for 1 minute, then scoop out and put into iced water. Squeeze the cooked spinach and herbs with your hands to get rid of as much water as possible.

Put all the ingredients, except the egg and the coconut oil, into a food processor. Add the egg gradually while pulsing the mixture into a rough paste (not too smooth). Using your hands, form the mixture into 12 small rounds and flatten each one slightly to form burgers.

Heat 2 tablespoons of coconut oil in a small, deep, non-stick frying pan—the oil should be approximately ⅛ inch deep. Working in batches, lay the green patties in the pan and lower the heat. Cook for 3 to 4 minutes on each side.

Serve the green burgers with a little green salad and the green sauce.

SPICED WINTER STEW WITH ORANGE BLOSSOM WATER, APPLE AND LIME

Perfect on its own or accompanied by meat or fish, this fragrant stew is just what a chilly winter's evening requires. Apple, orange, celeriac, artichoke—its flavors and textures deliver a much more interesting meal than a bowl of ready-made soup. It doesn't look very colorful, but it's delicious all the same.

INGREDIENTS

coconut oil
1 small celeriac, peeled and cut into
  3/8-inch cubes
3 parsnips, peeled and cut into
  3/8-inch cubes
5 ounces Jerusalem artichokes, peeled
  and cut into 3/8-inch cubes
1 large bulb of fennel, roughly chopped
1 large leek, white part only, roughly
  chopped
4 teaspoons Madras curry powder
sea salt
3 cups vegetable or chicken stock
1 Pink Lady apple, cored and
  cut roughly into chunks
2 teaspoons orange blossom water
juice of 1/2 a lime
freshly ground black pepper
chopped fresh parsley, to serve

Melt 2 tablespoons of coconut oil in a large casserole pan over low heat. Add the vegetables, curry powder, a pinch of salt and a ladleful of the stock. Simmer, covered, for 30 minutes until the vegetables are tender, stirring them a couple of times. Taste, and add more salt if needed.

Remove half of the vegetables to another pan and keep warm. Add the apple and the remaining stock to the vegetables in the first pan, then cover and simmer for 20 minutes, or until the apple is tender. Add 2 teaspoons of coconut oil and purée with a hand blender until you have a thick sauce—add a little more stock or water if needed. Add the orange blossom water and the lime juice and season.

Serve the vegetables with the sauce poured over and a sprinkling of fresh parsley.

STAGE ONE / *Spoon the ingredients into the pan*

STAGE TWO / *Break up the tuna*   **STAGE THREE /** *Crack the eggs*

STAGE FOUR / *Combine and cook*

STAGE FIVE / *Serve*

QUICK TUNA OMELET

This is a simple lunch that I pulled together one day when I was in a rush and had limited ingredients. It worked really well, so I thought I would share it with you all.

INGREDIENTS

olive oil
2 spring onions, finely chopped
1¾ ounces drained tuna (in brine, from a jar or canned)
¼ cup fresh tomatoes, roughly chopped and deseeded
3 large eggs, preferably free-range or organic
sea salt and freshly ground black pepper

Heat 1 tablespoon of olive oil in a non-stick pan and fry the spring onions for 2 to 3 minutes over medium heat. Stir in the tomatoes to heat through. Add the tuna, breaking it up with a fork, and fry for another minute.

Whisk the eggs in a bowl for 1 minute with a pinch of salt and some pepper.

Add the beaten eggs to the pan and lower the heat.

Wait for 1 minute, then, using a spatula, pull the omelet from the edge of the pan to the middle. Tip the pan slightly so that any uncooked mixture flows to the edges.

Cook for 2 to 3 minutes until the underside is set and lightly browned, then fold the omelet in half.

Serve with a green leafy salad and a classic vinaigrette.

CHICKEN AND TARRAGON CASSEROLE

This makes me think of my mum—she really rocks a casserole. It's something I used to be afraid to make, but thank goodness for the slow cooker! It really is a win-win solution. For me, this is pure joy in a bowl, at any time of the year.

INGREDIENTS

1 large, organic whole chicken,
   giblets removed
3 leeks, finely chopped
4 stalks of celery, finely chopped
4–6 carrots, peeled and chopped
1 large onion, finely chopped
1 clove of garlic, finely chopped
3 tablespoons raw almond butter
1 glass of white wine
juice and zest of 1 lemon
1 bunch of fresh tarragon, stalks
   removed and roughly chopped
sea salt and freshly ground
   black pepper

Put the chicken, leeks, celery, carrots, onion and garlic into a slow cooker and cook for 6 hours, or until the meat falls away from the bone (all slow cooker settings differ). If using an oven, cook for 4 hours at 325°F, but make sure to check regularly and ensure the ingredients are covered with liquid at all times. Add water if not. Once the chicken is cooked, remove it from the liquid and place in a dish to cool.

Meanwhile, add the almond butter, wine, lemon juice and tarragon leaves to the cooking liquid and vegetables. Season to taste. (You could also add some dried mushrooms here, and some other vegetables if you wish—if you do, replace the lid and cook for 10 to 20 minutes, or until cooked through.)

Shred the chicken meat, add it to the mixture and stir well. Sprinkle the lemon zest on top and serve either alone, with steamed greens, or with new potatoes (if you aren't watching your weight).

SPICED ROAST CHICKEN

For many people, roast chicken is one of the most-loved meals of the week. This recipe shows that a roast needn't be dripping in fat to taste amazing. Serve the chicken alongside spicy parsnip chips (see opposite) for a tasty, healthy alternative to a more traditional Sunday roast.

INGREDIENTS

1 whole organic chicken
   (approx. 3½ pounds, giblets removed)
2 red onions, peeled and quartered
1 lemon, halved
4 sprigs of fresh rosemary
3 tablespoons coconut oil, softened
3 cloves of garlic, peeled and
   finely chopped
1 teaspoon sweet smoked paprika
1 teaspoon ground turmeric
1 teaspoon ground cumin
sea salt and freshly ground black pepper
1 glass (approx. 6 ounces) dry white wine

Remove the chicken from the fridge 30 minutes before cooking and preheat the oven to 400°F. Put the chicken into an ovenproof dish just big enough to fit it. Push a quarter of the red onions into the cavity of the chicken and nestle the rest around it. Push the lemon halves into the cavity and add the sprigs of rosemary.

Make a paste with the coconut oil, garlic, paprika, turmeric and cumin. Season with salt and pepper. Ease the skin of the chicken away from the flesh with your fingers, creating a space for the spice paste. Using your fingers, ease half the spice mixture under the skin, rubbing it into the flesh. Slather the remaining half over the skin of the chicken. Pour the glass of wine into the dish along with the same quantity of water. Cook in the oven for 90 minutes, or until the chicken juices run clear. Rest for 15 minutes.

Serve the chicken with the pan juices, soft onions and parsnip chips. Steamed greens are always nice, too.

SPICY PARSNIP CHIPS

If you haven't tried the Middle Eastern spice called za'atar before, I urge you to find some and start cooking with it immediately! It lends an exotic flavoring that is hard to resist and which goes particularly well with roasted root vegetables, like parsnips.

INGREDIENTS

4 parsnips, peeled and cut into
 ¾-inch wedges
2 tablespoons olive oil
2 teaspoons macadamia nut oil
2 tablespoons za'atar, smoked paprika
 or garam masala
sea salt

Preheat the oven to 400°F. Fill a large pan with salted water. Add the parsnips and bring to a boil. Cook for about 4 minutes, until just tender. Put the olive oil and macadamia nut oil on to a large baking sheet and place in the oven to heat up.

Drain the parsnips, toss with the za'atar and a little sea salt, then take the baking sheet out of the oven and add the parsnips to it. Toss them in the oil and spread them out evenly. Cook until crispy, for about 1 hour, turning after 30 minutes.

Serve with a sprinkling of sesame seeds.

HERBY ZUCCHINI FRIES

Zucchini fries are a fabulous alternative to their often tricky-to-resist potato equivalent. Much easier to make than traditional fries and with a lovely delicate flavor, they're a deliciously moreish side dish and a real crowd-pleaser.

INGREDIENTS

2 medium zucchini
1 cup rice flour
2 tablespoons dried basil
2 tablespoons dried mint
2 tablespoons dried oregano
2 plump cloves of garlic, finely chopped
2 tablespoons sea salt
2 eggs, preferably free-range or organic
coconut oil

Start by cutting your zucchini into matchsticks. Cut off the tops and bottoms of the zucchini, then, using a mandolin set to about ¼ inch, slice them lengthwise. With a knife, slice the zucchini sticks lengthwise again, giving you very long, skinny fries.

Combine the flour with the dried herbs, chopped garlic and salt. Mix well and carefully pour onto a large plate. Whisk the eggs in a shallow bowl. Line a medium-size baking sheet with a dish towel.

Put 2 tablespoons of coconut oil into a large wok or frying pan and place over high heat. Dunk a large handful of the zucchini sticks in the egg mixture and toss to coat them. Transfer to the herby flour mixture and toss to coat again. Shake off any excess, then place the coated sticks in the hot pan. Cook for 2 minutes, then flip them over to brown the other side for 1 or 2 more minutes.

When crispy, transfer the fries to the lined baking sheet, add an extra tablespoon or two of oil to the pan, then heat and repeat the process until you have used up all the zucchini sticks.

Eat immediately, or keep warm in the oven set to low heat.

FISH STICKS WITH FAVA BEANS

Here's my take on a British classic. Use any variety of fish that appeals to you. I wanted to get the perfect crunch—obviously without using gluten, but also without using almond and coconut, which has been so overdone. So I was thrilled that this red lentil-based coating gives the perfect texture to these fish sticks. I love fava beans so created this mashed version as a different take on mushy peas.

INGREDIENTS

For the beans:
1 pound frozen fava beans, peeled (use fresh beans if it's the right time of year)
sea salt
a small bunch of fresh parsley
¼ cup chicken or vegetable stock
3 tablespoons olive oil

For the fish sticks:
¾ cup red lentils
1 teaspoon sea salt
¼ teaspoon freshly ground black pepper
½ teaspoon ground turmeric
¼ teaspoon ground coriander
zest of 1 lemon
1 large egg, preferably free-range or organic
10 ounces fresh cod fillet
coconut oil

Cook the fava beans in salted boiling water for 10 minutes. Drain, remove a handful and put to one side for later, then put the rest into a blender with the parsley. Add the stock and olive oil and blend until smooth. Mix in half of the reserved beans.

Pulse the red lentils in a heavy-duty food processor until you have a flour. Mix in the salt, pepper, turmeric, coriander and lemon zest then put on a deep plate or into a shallow bowl. Whisk the egg in another bowl.

Rinse the cod fillet, pat it dry with paper towels and cut into sticks. Dip the pieces of cod into the whisked egg and then into the red lentil mixture, making sure they are well coated on all sides. Place the coated pieces on a wire rack while you coat the rest.

In a small deep pan, heat 6 tablespoons of coconut oil and fry some of the fish sticks, making sure they are not touching each other. Cook for 2 to 3 minutes on each side or until golden brown. Transfer to a plate covered in paper towels while you fry the rest.

Serve the fish sticks and mashed fava beans with wedges of lemon and the remaining fava beans on top.

INDEX

Page references for recipe photographs are in **bold**

T

SOURCES

SUPPLIERS

For information and guidance on where to source some of the slightly more unusual ingredients in the book, please visit my website:

- *www.ameliafreer.com*

RESOURCES

All products used and mentioned in this book are available to purchase via my online shop:

- *www.ameliafreer.com*

WHERE I STUDIED:
The Institute for Optimum Nutrition (ION)
- *www.ion.ac.uk*

TO FIND A QUALIFIED NUTRITIONAL THERAPIST:
The British Association for Applied Nutrition and Nutritional Therapy (BANT)
- *www.bant.org.uk*

TO FIND A FUNCTIONAL MEDICAL PRACTITONER:
The Institute for Functional Medicine (IFM)
- *www.functionalmedicine.org*

ORGANIC BOX DELIVERIES
- *Abel & Cole www.abelandcole.co.uk*
- *Riverford Organics www.riverford.co.uk*

COOKING LESSONS:
Recipease
- *www.jamieoliver.com*

Leiths
- *www.leiths.com*

BOOKS:
- *Eat. Nourish. Glow.* by Amelia Freer
- *Grain Brain* by David Perlmutter, M.D.
- *Wheat Belly* by William Davis, M.D.
- *The Blood Sugar Solution* by Mark Hyman, M.D.
- *Nom Nom Paleo* by Henry Fong
- *The Optimum Nutrition Bible* by Patrick Holford

THANKS

I am so grateful to Louise Moore and Fenella Bates for welcoming me into the world of Penguin. Creating this book with such a dedicated, talented and passionate team has been a dream come true and what a great team effort it has been. My thanks to Fenella Bates, Lindsey Evans and Zoe Berville for their tireless guidance, support and friendship and to all of the rest of the team at Michael Joseph who have worked behind the scenes contributing to the creation of this book. Thanks to the many recipe testers, cooks and stylists on the never-ending shoot, especially to Anna Burges-Lumsden, Frankie Unsworth and Emma Lahaye.

I am especially grateful to John Hamilton for his skilled patience and for embracing my vision and ethos. It was a pleasure to work with someone who has such a respect for food and was able to interpret my philosophy and bring it to life on the pages.

And I'm hugely thankful to Susan Bell who was able to view all of the food as if through my own eyes and capture such elegant and edible photographs.

Thank you so much to George O'Dowd for contributing some recipes and taking time for a few photographs for this book and to Sam Smith who inspired a couple of the recipes—I feel very lucky to have the privilege of working with such lovely people.

Maria Lally once again helped me with my words and my good friend and fellow food snob, Christophe Reissfelder, made me laugh along the way and helped me to perfect my recipes.

Thank you Philippe Tholimet for sorting out my hair and Jo Frost for giving me make-up that didn't look like make-up.

A very special thank you to Krishna Montgomery and her team at Monty PR who have supported me in my career from the very beginning. Krishna has become a bit of a mentor, a bit of a manager and a good friend and I feel fortunate to be surrounded by her and her team. Good careers are made up of lots of good people.

My assistant Tania Smith has been a fantastic support and quietly manages the complicated day-to-day demands of my work. I am very grateful to her.

Thanks to my agent Elizabeth Sheinkman from William Morris Endeavour for helping my books get published and for introducing me to Karen Rinaldi at Harper Wave who has enabled my books to be published in the U.S.

This book is dedicated to my Mum, Lucy, who feared I might never cook and live only on Marmite and toast. But somehow she instilled her love for cooking and gift for it over the years and, although I came to it late, I hope this book does her proud.